KU-446-632

The **AA** POCKETGuide
CYPRUS

Original text by Robert Bulmer
Updated by George McDonald

© Automobile Association Developments Limited 2008
First published 2008
Reprinted July 2008

ISBN: 978-0-7495-5508-5

Published by AA Publishing, a trading name of Automobile Association Developments
Limited, whose registered office is Fanum House, Basing View, Basingstoke, Hampshire
RG21 4EA. Registered number 1878835.

Colour separation: Keenes, Andover
Printed and bound in Italy by Printer Trento S.r.l.

Front cover images: (t) AA/M Birkitt ; (b) AA/D L Day
Back cover image: AA/A Kouprianoff

A03876
Maps in this title produced from mapping © Freytag-Berndt u. Artaria KG,
1231 Vienna-Austria

About this book

Symbols are used to denote the following categories:

✚ map reference

✉ address or location

☎ telephone number

◷ opening times

✋ admission charge

🍴 restaurant or café on premises
or nearby

Ⓜ nearest underground train station

🚌 nearest bus/tram route

🚂 nearest overground train station

⛴ nearest ferry stop

ℹ tourist information office

❓ other practical information

↔ other places of interest nearby

▶ indicates the page where you will
find a fuller description

This book is divided into four sections.

Contents

Planning

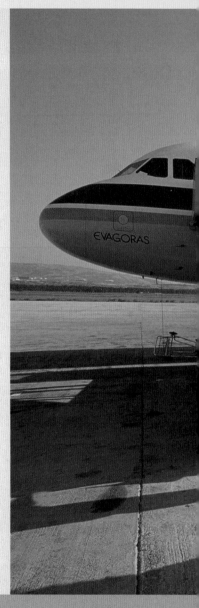

Before You Go

WHEN TO GO

JAN	FEB	MAR	APR	MAY	JUN	JUL	AUG	SEP	OCT	NOV	DEC
17°C	17°C	19°C	23C	26°C	30°C	32°C	33°C	31°C	27°C	22°C	19°C
63°F	63°F	66°F	73°F	79°F	86°F	90°F	91°F	88°F	81°F	72°F	66°F

🟦 High season   ⬜ Low season

Temperatures are the **average daily maximum** for each month on the south coast; there are small variations on the north, west and east coasts. In **Nicosia**, temperatures are approximately an average of 5°C (9°F) higher in summer and 5°C (9°F) lower in the winter; the **Troodos Mountains** are an average 10°C (18°F) cooler than the rest of the country.

The best weather for visiting the island is between March and May and September and November since July and August are very hot and dry.

In winter there are some warm spells, however they are often mixed with heavy rain. Snow usually falls in December and January in the Troodos Mountains.

WHAT YOU NEED

- ● Required
- ○ Suggested
- ▲ Not required

Some countries require a passport to remain valid for a minimum period (usually at least six months) beyond the date of entry – check before you travel.

	UK	Germany	USA	Canada	Australia	Ireland	Netherlands	Spain
Passport (or National Identity Card where applicable)	●	●	●	●	●	●	●	●
Visa (regulations can change – check before you travel)	▲	▲	▲	▲	▲	▲	▲	▲
Onward or Return Ticket	▲	▲	▲	▲	▲	▲	▲	▲
Health Inoculations (tetanus and polio)	▲	▲	▲	▲	▲	▲	▲	▲
Health Documentation (▶ 9, Health Advice)	●	●	●	●	●	●	●	●
Travel Insurance	○	○	○	○	○	○	○	○
Driver's Licence (national)	●	●	●	●	●	●	●	●
Car Insurance Certificate	○	○	n/a	n/a	n/a	○	○	○
Car Registration Document	●	●	n/a	n/a	n/a	●	●	●

ADVANCE PLANNING
WEBSITES
Cyprus Tourist Organization
www.visitcyprus.org.cy
North Cyprus Tourist Information
www.tourism.trnc.net

TOURIST OFFICES AT HOME
In the UK
Cyprus Tourist Office
17 Hanover Street, London
W1S 1YP ☎ 020 7569 8800

Northern Region of Cyprus Tourist
Information Office

29 Bedford Square,
London WC1B 3EG
☎ 020 7631 1930

In the USA
Cyprus Tourism Organization
13 East 40th Street
New York, NY 10016
☎ 212/683 5280

Northern Region of Cyprus Tourist
Information Office
1667 K Street, Suite 690,
Washington DC 20006
☎ 202/887 6198

HEALTH ADVICE
Insurance Tourists get free
emergency medical treatment;
other services are paid for. For UK
nationals benefits are available in
the Republic by arrangement with
the Department of Health before
departure. Medical insurance is
advised for all.

Dental services Dental treatment
must be paid for by all visitors.
Hotels can generally give
recommendations for local
dentists. Private medical insurance
is strongly advised to all tourists
to cover costs of dental treatment
in Cyprus.

TIME DIFFERENCES

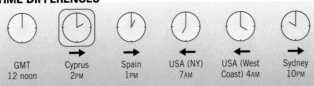

GMT	Cyprus	Spain	USA (NY)	USA (West Coast)	Sydney
12 noon	2PM	1PM	7AM	4AM	10PM

Cyprus is on Eastern European
Time from late March to late
October (GMT+2).

From late October to late March
the time is GMT+3.

WHAT'S ON WHEN

January
New Year's Day (1 Jan)
Epiphany (6 Jan): important Greek Orthodox religious celebration.

March
Greek National Day (25 Mar): parades and celebrations.

April
National Day (1 Apr): anniversary of the EOKA uprising.
National Sovereignty and Turkish Children's Festival (23 Apr).

May
Labour Day (1 May).
May Fair in Pafos (1 May): 10 days of cultural events; exhibitions of flora, basketwork and embroidery.
Anthestiria Flower Festivals (early May): the festivals' origins go back to celebrations honouring the god Dionysos in ancient Greece.
Turkish Youth Festival (19 May).
Cyprus International Fair (late May): the largest trade fair in Cyprus, held in Nicosia and lasting 10 days.

July
Larnaka Festival (throughout Jul): dance and theatre in the fort and the Pattichon amphitheatre.
Peace and Freedom Day (20 Jul): date of Turkish intervention in 1974, public holiday in the North.

August/September
Turkish Communal Resistance Day (1 Aug).
Turkish Victory Day (30 Aug).
Limassol Wine Festival (late Aug–first week in Sep): a 12-day festival, with music and dance.

October
Independence Day (1 Oct).
Greek National Day (28 Oct): also known as Ohi Day. Parades in the South.
Turkish National Day (29 Oct).

November
Proclamation of Turkish Republic of North Cyprus (15 Nov).

NATIONAL HOLIDAYS

JAN	FEB	MAR	APR	MAY	JUN	JUL	AUG	SEP	OCT	NOV	DEC
2		1	1(1)	1(2)	(1)		1		2		3

1 Jan	New Year's Day
6 Jan	Epiphany
25 Mar	Greek National Day
1 Apr	Cyprus National Day
Apr/May	Orthodox Easter
1 May	Labour Day
May/Jun	Pentecost/Kataklysmos (Festival of the Flood)
15 Aug	Assumption of Our Lady
1 Oct	Cyprus Independence Day
28 Oct	Greek National ('Ohi') Day
24–26 Dec	Christmas

Banks, businesses, museums and most shops are closed on these days.

December
Christmas Day (25 Dec).

Moveable feasts
Apokreo Festivities (50 days before Orthodox Easter): two weeks of fun. Limassol has fancy dress balls and children's parades.
Belapais International Music Festival (dates vary).
Green Monday (50 days before Orthodox Easter): a day of laughter, funny disguises and vegetarian picnics in the country.
Procession of Agios Lazaros Icon, Larnaka (eight days before Orthodox Easter Sun): a special Mass service in memory of Agios Lazaros followed by an impressive procession carrying his icon through the town.

Easter: the biggest Greek Orthodox religious feast – on the Sunday, celebrations last all day.
Kataklysmos, Festival of the Flood (50 days after Easter, coinciding with Pentecost): celebrations take place in all the seaside towns and include dancing, folk singing, swimming competitions and boat races.
Agia Napa Festival (late Sep): a weekend of folk music, dance and theatre, combined with agricultural exhibitions.
Seker or Ramazan Bayram: a three-day feast at the end of the Ramadan fast.
Kurban Bayram: four days during which lambs are traditionally sacrificed and shared with the needy.

Getting There

BY AIR
REPUBLIC OF CYPRUS

South Cyprus has two main airports, Larnaka and Pafos. Both are international airports and are served by the national airline Cyprus Airways (☎ 2236 5700; **www.**cyprusairways.com). The two airports and Limassol Harbour are the only recognized points of entry for international visitors.

If you travel to the North and are not a citizen of the European Union, you may be refused entry to the South.

Larnaka Airport is only 5km (3 miles) from the city centre. There is no bus service directly to and from the airport, but taxis are plentiful and inexpensive to Larnaka. If you are travelling to another town, consider taking a bus from Larnaka, otherwise your fare will be high.

Pafos Airport is 10km (6 miles) from the city and buses run six times a day between the city and airport. Taxis to the centre of Pafos are inexpensive, but onward taxi fares rise sharply. As with Larnaka, you might take a taxi to Pafos and continue your journey by bus.

NORTH CYPRUS

International flights arrive at Ercan Airport. There is no public transport from the airport, but taxis run to Nicosia, Keryneia and Famagusta.

BY SEA

Ferries arrive at either Keryneia or Famagusta harbours.

Getting Around

PUBLIC TRANSPORT
REGIONAL BUSES

Republic of Cyprus Intercity buses operate frequently between towns and various holiday resorts. Almost all villages are connected by local buses to nearest towns but services operate only on weekdays, once a day, leaving in early morning and returning in the afternoon.

North Cyprus Except for the main routes such as Nicosia to Keryneia (Girne), Famagusta (Gazimağusa) or Morfou (Güzelyurt), buses are infrequent, with no timetable.

BOAT TRIPS

Republic of Cyprus One-day boat excursions (usually including lunch) operate from April to October or November. Trips include Limassol Harbour to Lady's Mile Beach; Pafos Harbour to Coral Bay and Agios Georgios; Larnaka Marina along Larnaka, Agia Napa and Protaras; Agia Napa to Paralimni and Protaras; and Lakki along the Akamas coast.

North Cyprus From May to October there are boat trips (including lunch) from Keryneia (Girne) Harbour to the beaches at Acapulco and Alagadi, or to Alsancak, Lapta and Karşiyaka (☎ 815 3708).

URBAN TRANSPORT

Republic of Cyprus Urban and suburban buses operate frequently during the day between 5.30am and 7pm. During summer, in certain tourist areas, buses may operate until midnight. It is a good idea to check routes with your hotel.

North Cyprus There are good bus services within the main towns, with buses running approximately every half hour. Check with your hotel for more detailed information.

TAXIS

In the Republic service taxis, shared with other people (4 to 7 seats), operate between main towns every hour or so. There are also rural taxis that operate in hill resorts and urban taxis in towns.

In the North taxis can only be found at taxi stands.

CAR RENTAL

The many firms on the island include internationally known companies, though there are mainly local ones in the north. Cars, especially out of season, are moderately priced in the Republic and the North.

Drivers must usually be aged between 25 and 75 and have had a licence for more than a year.

CONCESSIONS

Students Cyprus is not really on the backpacker route, but there are youth hostels in Nicosia, Larnaka, Pafos and in the Troodos Mountains. For details contact: The Cyprus Youth Hostel Association, PO Box 24040, CY 1700 Nicosia (☎ 267 0027). The youth card 'Euro<26' secures discounts for ages 13–26 on a wide range of products. Contact the Youth Board of Cyprus, 62 Leoforos Aglantzias, Nicosia (☎ 2240 2600; **www.**Youthboard.org.cy).

Senior citizens Few concessions are made to elderly visitors. Most hotels offer discounts during the low season but these are available to all age groups.

DRIVING

Drive on the left.

Speed limits on motorways and dual carriageways:
100kph (62mph);
min **65kph (40mph)**.
Speed limits on country roads:
80kph (50mph) (North Cyprus: **65kph/40mph**).
Speed limits on urban roads:
50kph (31mph), or as signposted

Seatbelts must be worn in front seats at all times and in rear seats where fitted.

Random breath-testing takes place. Never drive under the influence of alcohol.

Fuel in the north and the Republic of Cyprus is less expensive than much of Europe. Grades sold are super, regular, unleaded and diesel. Fuel stations in the south open 6am–6pm, with automatic credit card/cash vending at other times. In the north they may open until 9 or 10pm.

If you break down in the Republic of Cyprus a 24-hour towing service is provided by the Cyprus Automobile Association in Nicosia (☎ 2231 3131), which is affiliated to the Alliance International de Tourisme (AIT).

If the car is rented follow the instructions given in your documentation.

Being There

TOURIST OFFICES

Republic of Cyprus
- Cyprus Tourism Organization
  PO Box 24535
  CY 1390 Nicosia
  ☎ 2269 1100
  www.visitcyprus.org.cy

- 11 Odos Aristokyprou
  Laïki Geitonia
  Nicosia
  ☎ 2267 4264
- 115A Odos Spyrou Araouzou
  Limassol
  ☎ 2536 2756
- 22 Odos Georgiou A'
  Germasogeia
  ☎ 2532 3211
- Plateia Vasileos Pavlou
  Larnaka
  ☎ 2465 4322
- 3 Odos Gladstonos
  Pafos
  ☎ 2693 2841
- 12 Leoforos Kryou Nerou
  Agia Napa
  ☎ 2372 1796
- Pano Platres
  ☎ 2542 1316
- 2 Odos Vasileos Stasioikou
  Polis
  ☎ 2632 2468

Northern Cyprus
- Nicosia
  ☎ 228 9629
- Keryneia
  ☎ 815 2145
- Famagusta
  ☎ 366 2864

EMBASSIES AND CONSULATES
UK
2286 1100 (RoC)
228 3861 (NC)
Germany
2245 1145 (RoC)
227 5161 (NC)
USA
2239 3939 (RoC)
227 8295 (NC)
Netherlands
2287 3666 (RoC)
Spain
2245 014 0 (RoC)

SUMMER OPENING HOURS (REPUBLIC)

● Shops ● Banks ● Museums
● Offices ● Archaeological sites ● Pharmacies

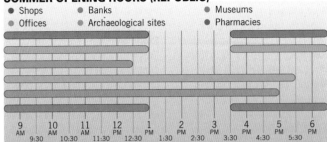

| 9 AM | 10 AM | 11 AM | 12 PM | 1 PM | 2 PM | 3 PM | 4 PM | 5 PM | 6 PM |
| 9:30 | 10:30 | 11:30 | 12:30 | 1:30 | 2:30 | 3:30 | 4:30 | 5:30 | |

SUMMER OPENING HOURS (NORTH)

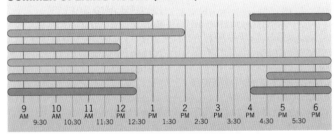

| 9 AM | 10 AM | 11 AM | 12 PM | 1 PM | 2 PM | 3 PM | 4 PM | 5 PM | 6 PM |
| 9:30 | 10:30 | 11:30 | 12:30 | 1:30 | 2:30 | 3:30 | 4:30 | 5:30 | |

TELEPHONES

In the Republic public telephones are found in town centres. They take coins or *telecards* (available in a variety of denominations from banks, post offices, tourist offices or kiosks). Payphones in the North now only accept phone cards, sold in denominations of 100, 200 and 300 units.

INTERNATIONAL DIALLING CODES

From Cyprus to
UK 00 44

USA 00 1
Netherlands 00 31
Spain 00 34
Germany 00 49

EMERGENCY TELEPHONE NUMBERS

Police assistance:
☎ 112 (Republic)
☎ 155 (North)
Fire:
☎ 112 (Republic)
☎ 199 (North)
Ambulance:
☎ 112 (Republic and North)

POSTAL SERVICES
Post offices
There are main post offices in main towns.
Republic: open Mon–Fri 7.30–1.30 (Thu also 3–6). Tel 2230 3219.
North: open Mon–Fri 8–1, 2–5, Sat 8.30–12.30. Tel 228 5982.

ELECTRICITY
The power supply is 240 volts
Type of socket: Square, taking three-square-pin plugs (as UK); in older buildings, round two-pin sockets taking two-round-pin (continental-style) plugs.

CURRENCY AND FOREIGN EXCHANGE
Currency: From 1 January 2008 the currency of the Republic is the euro. Coins are available in denominations of 1, 2, 5, 10, 20 and 50 cents and 1 and 2 euros; notes 5, 10, 20, 50, 100, 200 and 500 euros.

The currency of North Cyprus is the New Turkish Lira (YTL).

Credit cards and exchange:
Exchange travellers' cheques for Cyprus pounds or New Turkish Lira at banks, bureaux de change and hotels. Many banks have ATMs. Most currencies are accepted at banks, hotel exchanges and shops in both zones.

HEALTH AND SAFETY
Sun advice Cyprus enjoys almost constant sunshine all year. Wear a hat and drink plenty of fluids during the hot months (particularly July and August). A high-protection sunscreen is also recommended.
Drugs Minor ailments can be dealt with at pharmacies (*farmakio* in the south, *eczane* in the north). Pharmacies sell all branded medicines. Some drugs available only on prescription elsewhere are available over the counter.

TIPS/GRATUITIES

Yes ✓   No ✗

Hotels (service included)	✗	
Restaurants (service included)	✗	
Cafés/bars (service included)	✗	
Taxis	✓	10%
Tour guides	✓	€1
Porters	✓	€1 per bag
Hairdressers	✓	€1
Cloakroom attendants	✓	50c
Theatre/cinema usherettes	✗	
Toilets	✗	

Safe water Tap water in hotels, restaurants and public places is generally safe to drink though not very palatable in the north, particularly around Famagusta. Bottled water is widely available and inexpensive.

Personal safety The police are relaxed and helpful and English is widely spoken. In tourist areas in the south, Cyprus Tourism Organization representatives can provide a degree of assistance. However, crime in Cyprus is at a reassuringly low level. Take the usual precautions with regard to handbags and valuables left in cars. Any thefts or offences should be reported to the police, if only for insurance purposes.

● Do not try to cross the Green Line (the dividing line between the two parts) except at official crossing points.

● Keep away from military zones (north or south).

● Do not use roads marked as blocked-off on a map (they may encroach on military zones).

PHOTOGRAPHY
It is forbidden to photograph in both north and south near military camps or other military installations, in museums, and in churches with mural paintings and icons where a flashlight is required.

CLOTHING SIZES

France	UK	Rest of Europe	USA	
46	36	46	36	
48	38	48	38	
50	40	50	40	
52	42	52	42	
54	44	54	44	Suits
56	46	56	46	
41	7	41	8	
42	7.5	42	8.5	
43	8.5	43	9.5	
44	9.5	44	10.5	
45	10.5	45	11.5	Shoes
46	11	46	12	
37	14.5	37	14.5	
38	15	38	15	
39/40	15.5	39/40	15.5	
41	16	41	16	
42	16.5	42	16.5	Shirts
43	17	43	17	
36	8	34	6	
38	10	36	8	
40	12	38	10	
42	14	40	12	
44	16	42	14	Dresses
46	18	44	16	
38	4.5	38	6	
38	5	38	6.5	
39	5.5	39	7	
39	6	39	7.5	
40	6.5	40	8	Shoes
41	7	41	8.5	

Best places to see

1 Akamas Peninsula

A beautiful region of hills, valleys and rocky shores, ideal for rambling, with rich and varied flora and diverse wildlife.

This westernmost extremity is unique in the Greek Cypriot south of the island, not only for its beauty but also for the absence of tourist development. Three areas are now designated protected and no development is permitted. Proposals are still being discussed for the establishment of a national park.

The vegetation is Mediterranean, with large tracts of impenetrable *maquis* interspersed with a thin covering of pine trees and juniper. Autumn flowering cyclamen is everywhere. In places the landscape is impressively stark, with spectacular rock outcrops. On the beaches green and loggerhead turtles still come up to lay their eggs, and occasionally a monk seal may be sighted.

Although there are no metalled roads, the area is becoming popular with trail-bikers and walkers.

Several trails for ramblers have been created, starting at the Baths of Aphrodite, west of Polis. A network of marked paths traverses the hills and information panels outline the types of flora. These are described in a free booklet from the tourist office called *Nature Trails of the Akamas*. The ascent of Mouti tis Sotiras is worth contemplating: it only takes an hour to reach the summit and the view is superb. Needless to say, in summer it is a hot and sticky expedition. An alternative is to take a boat from Lakki for a swim and a picnic in one of the delightful coves, perhaps near Fontana Amoroza (Love's Spring), halfway to Cape Arnaoutis.

✚ 116 B1 ✉ Cyprus's westernmost peninsula 🍴 Baths of Aphrodite Tourist Pavilion Café (££) ❓ Across the road from the café, and at the end of a short path and under trees is the pool called the Baths of Aphrodite

2 Hala Sultan Tekke and Salt Lake

A Muslim holy shrine standing on the shore of a natural landmark, which has very different aspects in winter and summer.

For Turkish Cypriots, the Hala Sultan Tekke's importance is surpassed only by the shrines of

Mecca, Medina and al Aksha (Jerusalem). It was here that the prophet Mohammed's maternal aunt, Umm Haram, was buried in AD649. Apparently, she fell from a donkey and broke her neck while participating in an Arab raid on the island. Three enormous stones were raised to mark her grave and the site became an important place of pilgrimage for Muslims.

The mosque, with its distinctive dome and minaret, was built by the Turks in 1816, though the tomb dates from 1760. Visitors can enter the mosque but must respect the dress code and remove their shoes before entering.

In the summer the surrounding gardens are a relatively cool haven from the heat of the Salt Lake. This is a desert for much of the year, but in winter the lake fills with water and attracts a wide range of migrating birds. The most spectacular of the winter visitors are the flamingos, whose distinctive pink colour makes

an attractive sight, though their numbers have greatly reduced in recent years. In summer the water evaporates, leaving a dusty grey expanse that shimmers in the heat.

The salt was once a significant product in the island's economy, but today it is no longer economically viable to collect. It originates from the nearby sea, seeping up through the porous rocks during the rainy months.

✚ 119 D5 ✉ 3km (2 miles) west of Larnaka on the Kiti road ⏰ Jun–Aug daily 7.30–7.30; Sep–May daily 9–5 ✋ Free, but donation requested 🍴 Taverna (££) at car park 🚌 Bus from Larnaka with drop-off on the main road

3 Kourion

Kourion is the most important archaeological site in the Greek Cypriot south, impressively perched on the cliffs overlooking the sea.

There has been a settlement here since 3300BC, but the first major town was probably built by Mycenaeans around 1400BC. It reached its zenith under the Romans and it is their influence that is most evident from the ruins. It went into decline as it suffered from Arab raiders and the population moved inland. Excavations started in 1873 and have continued ever since.

The Theatre presents the most striking image of the whole site. It seated an audience of 3,500 and was probably built by the early Greeks and then extended by the Romans to allow for gladiatorial combat and for man against animal spectacles.

The Annexe of Eustolios lies just uphill from the Theatre and has an impressive mosaic floor. Further up the hill are the Baths, which also had mosaic floors. The Baths follow the Roman pattern, with a *frigidarium* (cold room), then a *tepidarium* (warm room) and a *caldarium* (hot baths). Mechanisms for heating the water, along with furnaces and tanks, are in evidence.

At the top of the hill west of the Theatre is the Building of the Achilles Mosaic. Constructed around a courtyard, it has a mosaic showing Achilles in disguise revealing his true identity to Odysseus by mistake. There is also a depiction of Ganymede and the Eagle. The house dates from about AD4. A similar house a short

distance down the track has a mosaic showing two gladiators in combat. Also visible are the remains of an aqueduct that brought the settlement's water supply to the Fountain House, traces of which can still be seen. Opposite the Fountain House is the Basilica, which was built in the 5th century. It has fragments of mosaics on the floor and the roof was once supported by 12 columns.

This site covers the main areas of interest, but about 1km (0.5 miles) towards Pafos is the openly accessible Stadium, which once seated 6,000.

✚ 117 E5 ✉ Off the Limassol–Pafos road ☉ Apr–May, Sep–Oct daily 8–6; Jun–Aug daily 8–7.30; Nov–Mar daily 8–5. Excavations on the site can close some parts at times Inexpensive 🍴 Café in the nearby tourist pavilion (£)
🚌 From Limassol ❓ Classical plays or productions of Shakespeare are performed through summer. The tourist office will have the programme

4 Kykkos Monastery

The monastery is the largest and richest religious foundation in Cyprus and is known throughout the Orthodox world.

Kykkos is high and alone in the hills of western Cyprus, but even at 1,318m (4,323ft) above sea level it is overlooked by higher ground. In summer its cloisters and courtyards are cool; in winter, when the mist descends, the temperature drops dramatically. Cypriots make pilgrimages to Kykkos from all over southern Cyprus, and hundreds may

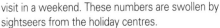

visit in a weekend. These numbers are swollen by sightseers from the holiday centres.

Kykkos was built about 900 years ago to house its icon, the painting of which is attributed to St Luke and was given to a Cypriot monk by Byzantine Emperor Alexius Comnenos for relieving his daughter's sciatica. The present construction is not of great antiquity – fires destroyed earlier buildings and nothing remain from before the 19th century.

In contrast with the spartan conditions of earlier times, today's monks have many modern comforts. Even so, the community has dwindled from hundreds to a handful, and even fewer novices.

The famous icon is called Eleousa. It has been encased in silver for 200 years and anyone attempting to gaze directly on it does so under sufferance of horrible punishment. Photography is not permitted. There is also a small one-room museum with items of interest from the monastery's past, mainly religious regalia and books.

In 1926 a novice called Michaïl Mouskos came to the monastery. He later became Archbishop Makarios III, and president of Cyprus. In those days he would be awake for prayers at 5.30am followed by a frugal breakfast. During the 1950s EOKA campaign the monastery was used by the guerillas for communications and the handling of supplies. Makarios is buried on the hill called Throni, directly above the monastery.

➕ 116 C4 ✉ West of Pedoulas, western Troodos
☎ Museum: 2294 2736 ⏱ Monastery: daily early morning to dusk. Museum: Jun–Oct daily 10–6; Nov–May daily 10–4
🎟 Free; museum inexpensive 🍴 Café nearby (£)

5 Lara

Lara is the name of a headland on the west coast with sandy bays on each side. This splendid stretch of coast continues up to Koppos Island, opposite which the rough road peters out, and then on to the distant northern cape.

The nearest outpost is Agios Georgios, hardly a village but having a church and harbour and restaurants. It sees the last of the hard surface road, and from now on the track is terrible, best attempted with a 4-wheel-drive vehicle or an off-road motorcycle . And there is quite a lot of it – 8km (5 miles) in all, with one steep area that is a real test of nerve on the cliff edge. Thicket, thorn and mimosa border the road, and only by chance or local knowledge can sandy coves on the rocky shore be found. The beaches of Lara itself are easier to discover, with a sweeping bay to the north and a smaller one to the south.

Lara is now a popular excursion destination and there are regular boat trips from Pafos, calling at

Agios Georgios on the way. Such splendid beaches and scenery would attract visitors in any circumstances, but there is a further incentive – Lara's famous sea turtles.

In an attempt to secure the future of these beleaguered and precious amphibians, a hatchery has been established at Lara. Its opening was accompanied by great publicity and many make the trip in the hope of seeing them; in fact there is no certainty of this – much depends on the cycle of the breeding season. The future of this beautiful and ecologically important coastline has been secured since the government declared that no building development was permitted in the area.

✚ 116 C1 ✉ Western Cyprus, north of Pafos 🍴 Café near the headland (£)

6 Nicosia Walled City

www.nicosia.org.cy

Eleven stout bastions superimposed on a circular wall give the city its distinctive and unique plan. Much has survived across the centuries.

Nicosia's formidable walls, so masterfully constructed by the Venetians, remain substantially intact, though Pafos Gate to the west is battered and Girne (Keryneia) Gate's situation ruined. Famagusta Gate has fared better, although it is now a cultural centre, perhaps something of a comedown for what was the important eastern entrance into the city. A lesser indignity has been

inflicted on the moat (always intended to be dry): this deep and formidable barrier to full-scale attack is now gardens, car parks and football pitches. In the end the great walls did not save Nicosia. The Turks broke through in 1570 after a bloody siege that lasted 70 days.

Today Lidras and Onasagoras streets, in the Greek Cypriot sector, are thriving places, and small shops are continuously busy. A little to the east the reconstructed buildings in the Laïki Geitonia quarter (► 91) are popular. In the Turkish Cypriot part development moves at a somewhat slower pace.

Along the backstreets some areas are conspicuously decrepit. This is not always to be regretted, as low overheads have enabled a Bohemian quarter to grow up around Famagusta Gate, with bars, cafés, a bookshop or two and a small theatre. Close by, and including Odos Ermou, is a renovated neighbourhood. The buildings, mainly houses, remain much as before, but have been refurbished. Small interesting squares, once rough underfoot, are now smoothly paved.

Of course, Nicosia is the city of the Green Line, a barrier of sandbags and barbed wire that can now easily be crossed at several official points, and was erected before the conscripts who now guard it were born.

➕ 126 B1 ✉ Centre of Nicosia 🍴 Cafés at Laïki Geitonia, Famagusta Gate, Atatürk Meydanı (£)

7 Pafos Mosaics

Roman houses with impressive and well-preserved mosaics depicting colourful scenes from Greek mythology.

The mosaics were discovered in five large 3rd century AD villas that probably belonged to wealthy Roman noblemen (one was presumably the governor's palace). The House of Dionysos was excavated first, after a passing shepherd turned up some fragments of mosaics. The depictions include Ganymede being taken to Olympus by an eagle. The most famous mosaic illustrates the triumph of Dionysos as he heads across the skies in a chariot drawn by leopards. According to the legend, Dionysos was the first person to discover how to make wine, and his followers are depicted enjoying the fruits of his labour.

The House of Aion displays a fine series of late 4th-century mosaics, which were discovered in 1983. The five scenes starting from the top left show Leda and the Swan; the baby Dionysos; then the middle panel portrays a beauty contest being judged by Aion; on the bottom row is the triumphant procession of Dionysos and the punishment of a musician, Marsyas, who had challenged Apollo to a musical contest and lost.

The House of Orpheus contains representations of Amazons, Hercules and the Lion of Nemea, alongside an impressive mosaic of Orpheus.

The main mosaic in the House of Theseus is that of Theseus killing the minotaur, although there are some others featuring Achilles and Neptune. The mosaics here are less well preserved than in other areas of the site. A newer discovery – the House of the Four Seasons – was unearthed in 1992. Mosaics showing the Gods of the Seasons and a variety of hunting scenes were found here. As excavations are continuing, parts of these houses may not be open to the public.

✚ 124 E1 ✉ Within the UNESCO World Heritage Site, a short distance inland from the harbour ☎ 2630 6217
🕒 Jun–Aug daily 8–7.30; Sep–May daily 8–5. Closed 1 Jan, 25 Dec, Greek Orthodox Easter Sun ✋ Moderate (includes Odeion ➤ 72 and Saranda Kolones ➤ 75)
🍴 Cafés at the harbour (££)

8 St Hilarion Castle

This fortified former monastery, besieged and taken by Richard the Lionheart in 1191, has spectacular coastal views.

Richard the Lionheart laid siege to the castle (Agios Ilarion), and after four days the Byzantine ruler Isaac Comnenos surrendered. Today the Turkish military controls the heights around the castle, and it is a significant place to advertise their presence.

This is no compact, easily visited site. There are lower, middle and upper wards, with quite a distance between each and a steep climb to the upper section. The big compensation for the effort – fairly substantial in the summer heat – is the unbelievable view. The north shore is directly below and mainland Turkey is plainly visible in the clear air of the cooler months. East and west a spectacular line of peaks and ridges runs into the distance.

St Hilarion, it seems, was a recluse who found refuge on these heights, and built a retreat here. A monastery was established on the site in the 11th century, and was later fortified and then extended by the Lusignans. The lower ward housed the garrison and their horses. A tunnel leads on to the middle ward and a small

Byzantine church. Some steps descend to a hall, which may have been a refectory, or banqueting chamber. Adjacent is a belvedere and café. The view over the coast is exceptional.

The path to the upper ward climbs steadily to the mountain top. Even then not everything is accessible, although St John's Tower, in its precipitous location, can be reached by a short detour. The Queen's Window is perhaps the ideal place to stop and rest.

✚ 120 C3 ✉ High in the hills west of Keryneia (Girne)
🕓 Jun–Sep daily 9–4.30; Oct–May daily 9–1, 2–4.45
🖐 Moderate 🍴 Café at the gate (£)

Salamis

In legend the founder of Salamis, an impressive archaeological site, was the Greek hero Teucer, brother of Ajax, and son of Telamon.

In the 7th century BC Salamis was the first city of Cyprus. It was not until the Roman occupation centuries later that it was succeeded by Pafos in the west. In AD350 the Byzantines changed the city's name to Constantia and restored it as the capital. There was much subsequent rebuilding due to earthquakes, but in the 7th century Arab attacks left the city in ruins.

In high summer a visit is a memorable occasion, although only the most determined will be able to stay the full course in the great heat. However, the Roman Theatre should not be missed, with its restored tiers of seats rising to an impressive height.

A little further north are the vents and hypocausts of the Baths, opening on to the Gymnasium, all built by the Romans. This structure, its rows of marble columns plainly evident, was damaged by earthquakes and remodelled in Byzantine times, only to collapse later. The columns that we see today were re-erected in the 1950s.

South of the Theatre the huge columns of the granite Forum lie across the site. To the east are the few remains of the church of Agios Epifanios, built in the 4th century. This northern section of the site was a cultural centre. The Agora is found in the

central part, near the Voutra, a 7th-century cistern. Close by are the ruins of the Temple of Zeus.

Walk of some 500m (550yds) northeast, towards the sea, and you will come to the Kampanopetra, a large Early Christian basilica, which has been only partially excavated. The Ancient Harbour is about 300m (330yds) southeast, on the shoreline. Alternatively, cross the main road and walk about 200m (220yds) to the western site. Here, at the Royal Necropolis, are several important tombs. These were designed for rich citizens, though there are also tombs for ordinary people nearby, called the Cellarka.

✚ 122 E3 ✉ 10km (6 miles) north of Famagusta (Gazimağusa) 🕐 Jun–Sep daily 9–7; Oct–May daily 9–1, 2–4.45 👋 Moderate 🍴 Café near north entrance (£)

10 Troodos Mountains

Despite their elevation, these are mostly rounded hills with a multitude of charming villages hidden in the pine-clad folds.

The Troodos is an extensive area, running from west of Larnaka to the high ground of Mount Olympos, then falling gradually to the western coast. There are many reasons for taking in the delights of the mountains, and they make a refreshing change from the hot beaches and dusty lowlands. Terraced vineyards shape the lower southern slopes, with Aleppo pine covering the higher ground. Summits may be tree covered or adorned with spiky scrub, relieved occasionally with dried flowers. Northern slopes are different again: dark poplars stand out in the valleys alongside golden oak and rock rose. Summer days are cooler on the high ground and a big attraction in winter is the snow, with skiing on Mount Olympos.

The most impressive of Cyprus's celebrated monasteries are in the Troodos. Chrysorrogiatissa (► 78–79), standing in splendid terrain, is about 45km (28 miles) from Pafos. Kykkos (► 28–29) is

more convenient for Limassol, but still half a day's excursion. In the east is Machairas (➤ 98–99), less splendid, but well worth a visit.

Regrettably few seek out the small Byzantine churches of Panagia tou Araka (➤ 100) and Stavros tou Agiasmati near Lagoudera on the north side of the range. This is understandable, because it is a long drive, but their frescoes are extraordinary.

Walks and trails are now popular in Cyprus, and those above Platres (Kalidonia Falls and around Mount Olympos) are detailed in a booklet produced by the tourist office. In western Cyprus the forest takes over, and Cedar Valley is renowned for its giant cedars. Fortunately for the peace of this marvellous area few people seem prepared to negotiate the difficult roads.

🔒 117 C5–7 ⊠ Central Cyprus 🍴 Cafés at Troodos resort, Platres, Foini, Kakopetria and other villages (£–££)

Exploring

In the south there are 340km (211 miles) of coast to explore, along with the fascinating Troodos Mountains and the towns of Larnaka (Larnaca), Limassol (Lemesos), Pafos (Paphos) and Nicosia (Lefkosia). Visitors in the north have to be content with long unspoiled shores, including the fabled Karpasia peninsula and the magnificent Pentadaktylos (Beşparmak) Mountains. The extensive Mesaoria plain is there for good measure.

The Cypriots have long had a reputation for being friendly and welcoming. This extra special reception is no longer common in the busy resorts and perhaps will soon be lost for ever, but it can still catch you unawares in a mountain village or the old quarter of Nicosia.

Larnaka and the Southeast

This part of Cyprus was once the agricultural heartland and it still provides the bulk of the Cypriot potato crop, which thrives in the distinctive red soil. However, in the last 20 years the agricultural industry has been supplanted by tourism, focused on two, previously quiet, resorts – Agia Napa and Protaras. The growth of these areas has been dramatic and Agia Napa today has around 20,000 tourist beds.

Beaches are the main attraction of this region, and the coastline offers a good range of places worth stopping at, although crowds tend to descend on summer weekends. The other attractions of the area are more low key: some traditional villages, Larnaka (Larnaca), the largest town, and a glimpse of the formerly 'forbidden city' of Famagusta (Gazimağusa).

Larnaka (Larnaca)

Larnaka is a significant tourist and commercial centre and is a convenient base for exploring the island, though its own places of interest are fairly limited. The modern city is built on the remains of ancient Kition, which was, according to the legend, established by one of Noah's grandsons in the 13th century BC. Out of this settlement Larnaka became an important trading centre, from where the island's main export of copper was shipped, and it has long had a large foreign population.

The town can be very busy at rush hour and the narrow streets and one-way system do not help the foreign driver. Visitors should try to park quickly and explore on foot. The pedestrianized seafront is lined with cafés and at the northern end of the promenade is a large marina with berths for 450 yachts. Larnaka is the main yachting centre of the island and the port facilities here attract boats from all over the eastern Mediterranean. There is a very popular beach, but it is man-made and is certainly not among the best on Cyprus. The seafront road provides amenities for tourists with an abundance of cafés, restaurants and ice-cream sellers.

Larnaka has a long history, but much of the evidence has been covered by the modern city. However the enthusiastic will be able

to track down archaeological remains and a few historic churches.

✚ 119 C5

AGIOS LAZAROS CHURCH

Legend states that St Lazarus, having been raised from the dead by Christ, came to Larnaka to live out the rest of his days and when he finally died he was buried here. His remains, however, were stolen and only his empty tomb is visible in the south apse. The church was built in the 9th century and restored in the

17th century, including the decoration of its extremely ornate interior. There is a small museum inside the building.

🕂 125 C3 ✉ Odos Agiou Lazarou ☎ Museum 2465 2498 🕔 Apr–Aug daily 8–12.30, 3.30–6.30; Sep–Mar daily 8–12.30, 2.30–5. Museum: closed Sun and Wed and Sat pm 👋 Museum: inexpensive

ARCHAEOLOGICAL MUSEUM

This museum has a good collection of exhibits – some date back to 3000BC – from Kition (➤ 48) and Choirokoitia (➤ 64). The first room contains statues and terracotta figurines. The pottery collection occupies the second room, along with some Mycenaean vases. Other rooms contain neolithic items, including a reconstruction of a tomb, and finally some Roman glassware. The garden fragments of statues and a mosaic pavement.

🕂 125 B3 ✉ Odos Kalograion ☎ 2463 0169 🕔 Mon–Wed, Fri 9–2.30, Thu 9–2.30, 3–5. Closed 1 Jan, afternoons Jul–Aug, 25 Dec 👋 Inexpensive
🍴 Cafés nearby (£)

KITION

The remains of the ancient city can be found at a number of sites.
The most visible ruins are on Leontiou Machaira near the
Archaeological Museum. The ditches and walls date from the 12th
and 13th centuries BC, when they enclosed the city. It is also
possible to make out the traces of a Phoenician temple, and the
sharp eyed may detect images of ships carved into the south wall.

✠ 125 B3 ✉ Odos Leontiou Machaira 🕐 Mon–Wed, Fri 9–2.30, Thu
9–2.30, 3–5. Closed afternoons Jul–Aug, 1 Jan and 25 Dec ✋ Inexpensive

PIERIDES MUSEUM

This museum was founded in 1974 to house the private collection of antiquities of Demetrios Pierides, covering the neolithic period to the Middle Ages. The collection, of 3,600 exhibits, is displayed

in the Pierides family's fine 19th-century house, and contains early pottery decorated with various designs, items from the site at Marion, mainly jugs and vases, and one of the most important collections of Roman glassware and jewellery in Europe. The main hall has some early maps of Cyprus and traditional folk artefacts.

✚ 125 C3 ⊠ Odos Zinonos Kitieos ☎ 2481 7868 ◉ Mon–Thu 9–4, Fri, Sat 9–1. Closed 1 Jan, 25 Dec, Greek Orthodox Easter Sun ✋ Moderate ✖ Cafés nearby (£)

TURKISH FORT AND MEDIEVAL MUSEUM

The fort was built in 1625 by the Turks to defend the city against

raiders but was soon adapted for use as a prison. It now contains a small medieval museum, featuring mainly suits of armour. There are also some artefacts from Kition (➤ opposite) and other excavations in the area. In summer

theatrical performances sometimes take place in the courtyard.

✚ 125 C3 ⊠ Larnaka seafront, south end of Odos Ankara ☎ 2430 4576 ◉ Jul–Aug Mon–Fri 9–7.30; Sep–May Mon–Fri 9–5. Closed 1 Jan, 25 Dec ✋ Inexpensive ✖ Cafés nearby (££)

What to See in the Southeast

AGIA NAPA

This major resort stretching along the coast has a reputation for clubs and bars. The town centre retains some appeal with its monastery and adjoining square, and the beaches are excellent, but crowded in summer.

Agia Napa Monastery and its gardens are a welcome haven. Its church was built in the 16th century over a cave where an icon of the Virgin Mary was supposedly found. Within a century the monastery had grown rich, owning much land. It was abandoned in the 18th century but later restored under British rule.

The exhibits at the **Marine Life Museum** include a large number of fossils and shells from Cyprus's waters. A reconstruction of the seabed displays turtles and sharks. One section features marine fauna of the late Cretaceous period and even shows dinosaurs.

Among the sculptures, engravings, vases and ceramics at the **Museum of the Sea** is a full-size replica of the ancient ship

Kyrenia 2 and a papryrus vessel of 9200BC. The museum also has art exhibits and hosts concerts.

✚ 119 C7

Monastery

✉ Centre of Agia Napa village ⏱ Daily ✋ Free 🍴 Many cafés nearby (££)

Marine Life Museum

✉ 25 Odos Agias Mavris
☎ 2372 3409
⏱ Mon–Wed, Fri–Sat 9–2; Tue 9–2, 3–6 ✋ Moderate
🍴 Many cafés nearby (££)

Museum of the Sea

✉ Town Square opposite the monastery ⏱ Tue–Wed, Fri–Sat 9–2; Tue 9–2, 3–6 ✋ Moderate 🍴 Café in complex

DERYNEIA

This village gives an insight into recent Cypriot history. It is the nearest settlement to Famagusta and one villager has set up a viewing point where tourists, for a small fee, can climb up to the roof of his house and look through a telescope across to the closed Famagusta suburb of Varosha.

✚ 119 B7 ✉ 11km (7 miles) north of Agia Napa 🍴 Café in village (£), restaurant on road to Paralimni (££) 🚌 From Protaras, in summer every hour 8–3, Sun last bus 1.30

HALA SULTAN TEKKE AND SALT LAKE

See page 24–25.

NISSI BEACH

Nissi Beach is where tourist development in this area started. It is

a pleasant sandy beach, though it can be very crowded in summer, with a rocky island just offshore. The presence of a sand bar makes it possible to wade to the island, an adventure that appeals especially to children. Those going to the island should, however, bear in mind that it is made up of rough

and spiky rocks and suitable footwear is necessary.

➕ 119 C7 ✉ 2km (1 mile) west of Agia Napa 🍴 Several cafés (£)

PANAGIA ANGELOKTISTI CHURCH
(KITI CHURCH)

Panagia Angeloktisti, which means 'built by angels', was constructed in the 11th century on the remains of a 5th-century church. It has many ornate icons but its main attraction is a mosaic that depicts angels attending the Virgin Mary as she holds Christ; it is a very intricate composition, of a style not found elsewhere in Cyprus. The mosaic will be lit up for visitors on request.

➕ 118 D4 ✉ Edge of the village on road to Mazotos ☎ 2442 4646 ⏱ Daily 8–12, 2–4. If locked ask for the key at the nearby café ✋ Donation requested 🍴 Café nearby (£) 🚌 From Larnaka

POTAMOS TOU LIOPETRI

This pleasant creek serves as a small fishing harbour. At the shoreline there is a taverna and a long, if slightly rocky, beach with the church of Agios Georgios at its western end. Early in the morning, when the fishermen are returning with their catch, it is a lovely place. The beach is usually quiet and provides an opportunity for calm, safe swimming.

➕ 119 C7 ✉ 14km (8.5 miles) west of Agia Napa 🍴 Taverna on beach (££)

PROTARAS

Protaras, also known as Fig Tree Bay because of a fig tree that was once its only landmark, is a fully fledged resort full of hotels, restaurants and dance clubs. The beach is sandy and there are good water sports facilities. The offshore rocky islet offers the chance of some small degree of seclusion although you have to be a fairly strong swimmer to reach it.

🚹 119 B8 ✉ 8km (5 miles) north of Cape Gkreko (Greco) on east coast 🍴 Numerous cafés and restaurants (£–££) 🚌 From Agia Napa in summer: every hour 9–5, Sun 10–5

STAVROVOUNI MONASTERY

The monastery of Stavrovouni, at an altitude of 690m (2,263ft), has spectacular views from the top of the hill. There has been a religious community here since AD327 when St Helena brought a fragment of the True Cross from Jerusalem. It is claimed that the piece is still in the monastery, covered by a silver casing. The original buildings were destroyed by Arab and Turkish raiders and those visible today date mainly from the 17th century. They are still occupied by a devout community of monks and women are not allowed inside.

🚹 118 D3 ✉ 40km (25 miles) west of Larnaka 🕐 Men only. Apr–Aug daily 8–12, 3–6; Sep–Mar daily 8–12, 2–5 ✋ Free

Limassol and the Southwest

This region has something for all tastes and all interests: an attractive coastline, a medieval castle, spectacular views, archaeological sites and, for the mythologically or romantically inclined, the birthplace of Aphrodite.

Anyone interested in history will find plenty to occupy them. The 9,000-year-old site at Choirokoitia is the oldest settlement on the island, while Kourion and its restored amphitheatre has relics from the Mycenaean, Persian and Roman periods. There are links with mythology too – a temple to Apollo – and, at Petra tou Romiou, the place where Aphrodite is said to have emerged from the foaming sea. A newer tradition, only 500 years old, is found in the lacemaking village of Lefkara, and beyond Limassol (Lemesos) are the vital ingredients for any Cypriot holiday, some good beaches.

Limassol (Lemesos)

Limassol's main claim to fame is that England's Richard the Lionheart was shipwrecked here and married his fiancée Berengaria in the town. The Knights Hospitaller developed Limassol as a trading post based on export of the Commandaria wine, which they made from the vineyards surrounding Kolossi. However, it was only in the 19th century that its major asset, the deep-water port, began to be appreciated and the town became a significant commercial centre.

In recent years Limassol has seen massive tourist development along the wide and noisy approach road on a stretch of coast without good beaches. It is a modern town but it does not lack atmosphere and has good shopping, nightlife and restaurants. The carnival in spring and the wine festival in early September are particularly lively times to visit the town.

The sights of Limassol are easily explored on foot, indeed cars encounter traffic problems and a fiendish one-way system. The main historical sight is the castle and medieval museum. There are also a couple of mosques – reminders of Limassol's Turkish quarter. The main shopping area is around Odos Agiou Andreou.

✚ 117 E7

AMATHOUS

These archaeological remains are spread widely and include a rock-cut tomb in the grounds of the Amathus Beach Hotel. The most easily accessible ruins are of the Agora, in a fenced site just off the main road on the inland side. This was the market area and though it is a relatively small site many pillars are still visible, which make it quite an impressive place. Up a track from the Agora is the Acropolis and remains of a Temple to Aphrodite. There is evidence that some of the site lies underwater, which offers interesting opportunities for snorkellers and scuba-divers.

✚ 117 E7 ✉ 8km (5 miles) east of Limassol ☻ Apr–May, Sep–Oct daily 9–6; Jun–Aug daily 9–7.30; Nov–Mar daily 9–5 ♨ Inexpensive 🚌 From Limassol and Larnaka

CASTLE AND CYPRUS MEDIEVAL MUSEUM

The main buildings of the castle were constructed in the 14th century on the site of an earlier Byzantine fortification. The chapel in which Richard the Lionheart and Berengaria were married was part of the original castle but is no longer standing. The castle was occupied by the Turks and later used by the British as an army headquarters.

The Cyprus Medieval Museum is now housed here. The basement contains replicas of sculptures and photographs of the Byzantine churches of Cyprus. Upstairs the exhibits are in small rooms off a central hall, with the most memorable items – armour and weapons – on the second floor. The final flight of stairs leads out on to the battlements, from where there are good views of the city. The most distinctive sights on the skyline are the two mosques, Cami Djedid and Cami Kebir, reminders that this was once the Turkish part of town.

✚ 125 F2 ✉ Odos Eirinis, near the old harbour ☎ 2530 5419 🕐 Mon–Sat 9–5, Sun 10–1. Closed 1 Jan, 25 Dec 🖐 Inexpensive 🍴 Many cafés nearby (£)

DISTRICT ARCHAEOLOGICAL MUSEUM

The garden contains a sundial that supposedly belonged to the British Lord Kitchener. Inside, Room 1 contains neolithic tools and pottery from Amathous (➤ 58) and Kourion

(➤ 26–27). These artefacts are very old, with some dating back to 2300BC. Room 2 has later figurines and Roman coins. The final room contains statues from Amathous including those of Artemis and the Egyptian god Bes.

✚ 125 D4 ✉ Corner of Odos Kanningos and Odos Vyronos ☎ 2530 5157 🕐 Mon–Fri 10–5, Sat 10–1. Closed 1 Jan, 25 Dec, Greek Orthodox Easter Sun 🖐 Inexpensive

MUNICIPAL GARDENS AND ZOO

The Municipal Gardens provide some welcome greenery in a dusty city. They also contain a small zoo, though the animals are kept in poor conditions. There is a small open-air theatre, where productions are held during the summer. The gardens are also the site of the annual Limassol Wine Festival, held in September. All the local wine companies set up stalls and have an evening of free wine tasting accompanied by music and dancing.

✠ 125 D4 ✉ Odos Oktovriou 28 ☎ 2558 8345 ◉ Gardens: daylight hours. Zoo: daily 9–6.30 ✋ Gardens: free. Zoo: moderate ⑪ Café in the Gardens (£)

What to See in the Southwest

AKROTIRI PENINSULA

The area contains a good beach, a salt lake and a historic church. In summer the salt lake is dry, has a grey colour and you can smell the salt; in winter it fills with water and is a stopping off point for passing flamingos. Lady's Mile Beach is sandy and has safe

swimming in the shallow sea. The far end is closed off, marking the start of the British base at Akrotiri – the occasional military jet may disturb the peace.

The monastery of **Agios Nikolaos ton Gaton** (St Nicholas of the Cats) is reached on a track at the southern end of the beach. It was founded in AD325, though the buildings seen today were constructed in the 13th century and have been restored since. The cats in the name are still much in evidence.

✚ 117 F6

Agios Nikolaos ton Gaton

⊙ Daily. Closed during mid-afternoon 🖐 Free 🍴 Cafés on beach (£)

AVDIMOU BEACH

Avdimou Beach is a good long sandy stretch, though the water becomes deep very quickly. There is a small taverna at each end and it is usually quiet, but at weekends it can be busy with service personnel and their families. It is part of the British Sovereign Base and so has not seen any tourist development.

✚ 117 E5 ✉ 3km (2 miles) off main road, opposite turning to Avdimou village 🍴 Taverna on beach (£)

CHOIROKOITIA

This is the oldest archaeological site on the island, dating from 6800BC when 2,000 people lived here and farmed the surrounding land.

The beehive-shape houses that define the settlement, come in two sizes, one about 4m (13ft) across and the other 8m (26ft). They were built close together and linked by narrow passage-ways, and it was apparently crowded. The inhabitants tended to bury their dead under the floor of the house and then build on top, and some houses have revealed up to eight different periods of occupation.

The settlement is best explored by following the vestiges of

the main street, with House A near the entrance being the easiest to make out. A second group of ruins has the remains of pillars visible which once supported the roof. From there the site becomes more complicated and the best views are from the top of the hill, from where the wider perspective can reveal its layout.

✚ 118 D2 ✉ Off Junction 14 Nicosia–Limassol motorway ☎ 2432 2710
🕐 Apr–May, Sep–Oct daily 9–6; Jun–Aug Mon–Fri 9–7.30, Sat–Sun 9–5; Nov–Mar daily 9–5. Closed 1 Jan, 25 Dec, Greek Orthodox Easter Sun
👋 Inexpensive

KOLOSSI CASTLE

Kolossi was the headquarters of the Knights Hospitaller, who built the first castle in the late 13th century. They exploited the land here, using local sugar and grapes to make Commandaria wine.

The castle suffered from a number of attacks by Egyptian Mameluke raiders in the 14th century, and the buildings visible today date from a rebuilding that took place in the 15th century. The Turks took it over in 1570 and sugar production continued until 1799. Visitors pass over a drawbridge into a pleasant garden and then into the keep, which has thick wall and rises to three storeys.

Much of the ground floor was used as a storage area. The first floor has two large rooms and a kitchen. On the top floor were the apartments of the Grand Commander. A spiral staircase leads onto the roof, from where there are good views.

➕ 117 E6 ✉ 14.5km (9 miles) from Limassol ☎ 2593 4907 🕐 Apr–May, Sep–Oct daily 9–6; Jun–Aug daily 9–7.30; Nov–Mar daily 9–5 ✋ Inexpensive 🍴 Cafés nearby (£–££)

KOURION

See pages 26–27.

LEFKARA

The village is divided into Pano (upper) and Kato (lower) Lefkara, and is a very popular tourist destination. Visitors who prefer to avoid the crowds come in the early morning.

Lefkara is known for its lace, called *lefkaritika*; it first became famous in 1481 when Leonardo da Vinci supposedly ordered some for Milan Cathedral. The lace then became popular with Venetian ladies and the lacemaking industry took off. The tradition continues to flourish and rather ferocious ladies will offer their wares vigorously to passing tourists. Those wishing to buy should take care to ensure that it is the genuine article and not imported. There are also a number of silverware shops.

The main street of Pano Lefkara is now designed to cater for tourists but the narrow alleys to either side are still peaceful places to wander. There is also a small **museum** of lacemaking and silverware, signposted uphill from the main street.

The lower half of the village is often neglected but is worth a visit. Its church of Archangel Michael has some beautiful 18th-century icons and there are good views across the hills from outside the building. The distinctive houses in this part of the village are painted blue and white and its streets are extremely narrow and therefore traffic free.

➕ 118 D2 ✉ 9km (5.5 miles) northwest of junction 13 of the Nicosia–Limassol motorway 🍴 Cafés in the main street of the upper village (£)

Museum

☎ 2434 2326 🕐 Mon–Thu 9.30–4, Fri–Sat 10–4 ⚐ Inexpensive

PETRA TOU ROMIOU (ROCK OF APHRODITE)

This is one of the most photographed sites on the whole island. The name means the Rock of Romios and the two large rocks in the sea, set against the white cliffs, provide a spectacular scene. There are two official places to stop – one close to the rock, just back from the shore, where there is a café and a car park, the other higher up in the cliffs, where there is a tourist pavilion. However, the best view, coming from Limassol, is on the final bend before the road starts to descend; some scrubland on the left makes a convenient stopping place.

Legend states that this was the birthplace of Aphrodite, where she emerged from the water. The beach itself is shingly, and it is not ideal for swimming because it gets rough around the rocks, but it is worth stopping to soak up the mysterious atmosphere.

✚ 116 E3 ✉ 24km (15 miles) east of Pafos 🍴 Two cafés, one in the tourist pavilion (£)

SANCTUARY OF APOLLO YLATIS

The temple was first used in the 8th century BC, though the present ruins date from AD100, when it was rebuilt after an earthquake. There is a waymarked path and map to guide the visitor around the site. The circular remains of a votive pit are worth a closer look. The pit was used to store unwanted ritual gifts and archaeologists have found it a rich source of artefacts. The path then leads to the Temple of Apollo, which has been partially restored, its high columns a striking reminder of ancient times. A shed structure covers the Priest's House, and though you have to peer through the fence you can see some mosaics and pillars.

The remaining buildings of interest are the Palaestra, which was an open space used for sporting activities, and a nearby complex of baths.

🚹 117 E5 ✉ Limassol–Pafos road ☎ 2599 7049 🕐 Apr–May, Sep–Oct daily 9–6; Jun–Aug daily 9–7.30; Nov–Mar daily 9–5. Closed 1 Jan, 25 Dec, Greek Orthodox Easter Sun ✋ Inexpensive

Pafos and the West

This is the region for those looking for some of Cyprus's quieter and more traditional areas. However, Pafos (Paphos) continues to expand greatly and has cast off its small town origins, although not its important archaeological heritage. In the north are monasteries and villages. Polis, the only town of any size on the north coast, is no longer as laid-back as it once was. In the far northwest is the Akamas peninsula, which is the focus of environmental initiatives to protect some of the most remote and beautiful landscapes in Cyprus. East of Polis is an undeveloped region with empty beaches and quiet roads up to the Green Line that marks the limit of easy exploration for visitors in the Greek Cypriot sector of the island.

Pafos (Paphos)

The first settlement dates from the 4th century BC and Pafos played an important role in early Cypriot history. After the 4th century AD it declined and, though its fortunes improved marginally under British administration, it is only in the last 30 years, as transport links improved, that Pafos has seen real growth. Tourist development, in particular, took off after the construction of the international airport in 1983. The richness of its archaeology has qualified ancient Nea Pafos as a UNESCO World Heritage Site.

The town is split into upper and lower Pafos, known as Kitma and Kato Pafos. The lower part, on the coast, contains most of the historic sites whereas the upper town contains the main commercial centre, shops and modern museums. It is quite a strenuous walk between the two parts of town. The lower town contains a number of archaeological sites. Some are in formal areas, but you might come across ancient ruins among modern houses. The harbour is the focus of the lower town and is a pleasant place to stroll. Cafés string out along the seafront and there are plenty of places to eat or have a drink, although it can be very busy at the height of the season.

✚ 116 D2

CATACOMBS

There are two underground churches in Pafos. Agia Solomoni is easily identified because those who believe in the magical curative powers of the tomb attach items of clothing to the tree outside.

The underground chambers include a 12th-century chapel with frescoes, some of which are damaged by water and early graffiti by passing crusaders. The chambers are dark and a torch is useful, though the main chapel is lit by candles.

The second catacomb, a few minutes walk north, is larger, but has been less well cared for.

✠ 124 D2 ✉ Leoforos Apostolou Pavlou ⏰ Daylight hours ✋ Free

DISTRICT ARCHAEOLOGICAL MUSEUM

The museum houses most of the finds from local excavations. In the entrance hall is a Hellenistic sarcophagus from Pegeia and there are pottery and terracotta figures from Polis. There are also small statues and artefacts from the House of Dionysos, and sculpture and coins from the ancient city kingdoms of Cyprus. Most fascinating are articles found in Room 3, including marble Roman eyeballs and clay hot-water bottles.

✠ 124 C4 ✉ Leoforos Georgiou Griva Digeni ☎ 2630 6215 ⏰ Mon–Fri 9–4, Sat–Sun 9–1. Closed 1 Jan, 25 Dec, Greek Orthodox Easter Sun ✋ Inexpensive 🍴 Cafés across the road (£)

ETHNOGRAPHICAL MUSEUM

This private collection of George Eliades, a local professor, ranges from neolithic to modern times. The collection includes axe heads, coins, pottery and farm implements from around the island. There is also a reconstruction of a bridal chamber displaying traditional costumes and furniture.

✠ 124 C3 ✉ 1 Odos Exo Vrisis ☎ 2693 2010 ⏰ Mar–Nov Mon–Sat 9–5, Sun 10–1; Dec–Feb Mon–Sat 9.30–5, Sun 10–1 ✋ Inexpensive 🍴 Cafés nearby (£)

ODEION

This theatre has been partially restored to give an impression of how it would once have been. It was built in the 2nd century AD, during the Roman period, then suffered earthquake damage in the 7th century and was abandoned. Occasional performances are held here during the summer and details are available from the tourist office. Just in front of the Odeion is the Agora, once the city's market place. The foundations and some of the columns survive, and there are remains of some other municipal buildings.

✚ 124 D1 ⊠ Within the World Heritage Site, a short distance inland from the harbour ⏰ Jun–Aug daily 8–7.30; Sep–May daily 8–5 💷 Moderate, including Mosaics and Saranda Kolones 🍴 Cafés (£) nearby

PAFOS FORT

Originally the harbour was guarded by two castles built by the Lusignans in the 13th century. Both were badly damaged when the Turks attacked in 1570, but one was subsequently restored and used by the Turks as a prison. It is open to the public and you approach across a drawbridge. The main attractions are the dungeons and battlements, from where there are excellent views.
➕ 124 E1 ✉ Harbour Wall ☎ 2693 2841 🕐 Jun–Aug daily 10–6; Sep–May daily 10–5. Closed 1 Jan, 25 Dec, Greek Orthodox Easter Sun ✋ Inexpensive
🍴 Cafés on harbour front (££)

PAFOS MOSAICS

See pages 34–35.

ST PAUL'S PILLAR AND AGIA KYRIAKI

This is a small archaeological site in the back streets of Pafos, where a large number of columns and other fragments remain from the early Christian Basilica of Agia Kyriaki. Excavations are still taking place and this may mean that parts of the site will be closed off. Most people come here to see St Paul's Pillar, which stands at the western end of the  site. According to legend, St Paul was tied to this stone and given 39 lashes as a punishment for preaching Christianity. Despite this early setback, he later managed to convert the governor, and the rest of the island soon followed suit.

The adjacent church of Panagia Chrysopolitissa dates from the 12th century and is still used for services.
➕ 124 E2 ✉ Odos Stassandrou 🕐 Daylight hours ✋ Free
🍴 Cafés nearby (£)

SARANDA KOLONES (FORTY COLUMNS) BYZANTINE FORT

This castle dates from around the 7th century, although it was rebuilt in the 12th century, probably to protect the city from seaborne raiders until it was replaced by the forts on the breakwater. The remains of many of the original columns, the central keep and some of the towers on the thick outer walls can still be made out. You can also see a horse-trough and ancient latrines. The site is completely open and you can scramble around the ruins, but take care if you have young children.

✚ 124 E2 ✉ Within the World Heritage Site, a short distance from the harbour 🕐 Jun–Aug daily 8–7.30; Sep–May daily 8–5 ✋ Moderate, including mosaics and Odeion 🍴 Cafés nearby (££)

TAFON TON VASILEON (TOMBS OF THE KINGS)

The 100 tombs on the site cover a wide area and are cut out of the ground with a steep drop into them, so take care when exploring. Steps lead down inside the tombs, often into a whole series of passageways. The chambers near the centre of the site get busy and it is worth walking a little further to those on the edge of the area, which are just as impressive. They are constructed with Doric columns, date from about the 3rd century BC and were probably used to bury members of local noble families.

There are some good views over the sea and a few coves are accessible.

✚ 124 B1 ✉ Leoforos Tafon ton Vasileon, 2km (1 mile) northwest of Pafos ☎ 2630 6295 🕐 Apr–May, Sep–Oct daily 8–6; Jun–Aug daily 8–7.30; Nov–Mar daily 8–5 ✋ Inexpensive 🍴 Café on site (£) 🚌 10, 15 from Pafos

What to See in the West

AGIOS GEORGIOS

Agios Georgios is a pleasant harbour with a handful of restaurants, a small cluster of hotels and rooms to rent. The whole area was once a Roman settlement and some of the tombs cut out of the rock can be seen. On the headland are the remains of a 6th-century basilica.

The harbour is reached down a track from the headland and signposted Mandoulis beach. It is a very pretty place with a good stretch of sand and a view to the rocky island of Geronisos.

✚ 116 C1 ✉ 25km (15.5 miles) north of Pafos 🍴 Restaurants overlooking the harbour (£)

AGIOS NEOFYTOS MONASTERY

Saint Neofytos set up residence in caves he cut out of the hillside in 1159. The first cave he created was called the *enkleistra*, or enclosure. He then enlarged the dwelling with the addition of three new chambers, which are decorated with religious wall paintings focusing on the Crucifixion and Resurrection. Those in the sanctuary, the cave with an altar, are the best preserved. The 16th-century monastery church is dedicated to the Virgin Mary and contains a large number of paintings that depict her early life. Neofytos's bones are also kept here in a wooden sarcophagus, with his skull in a silver reliquary, which the devoted queue up to kiss.

✚ 116 D2 ✉ 9km (5.5 miles) north of Pafos 🕐 Apr–Oct daily 9–12, 2–4; Nov–Mar daily 9–4 ✋ Inexpensive 🍴 Café outside monastery 🚌 Two buses a day from Pafos lower town

AKAMAS PENINSULA

See pages 22–23.

CHRYSORROGIATISSA MONASTERY

The monastery is impressive mainly because of its setting at a height of 610m (2,000ft). It was founded in 1152 by a monk called Ignatius, although the main part of the monastery was not built until 1770. These buildings were burned down in 1821 when the Turks suspected the monks of political activity. Further trouble came in the 1950s when the abbot was murdered by EOKA terrorists who thought, erroneously, he had betrayed some of their comrades.

The current abbot has shown much enterprise in reopening an old winery and the monks now produce and sell some excellent wines. A collection of icons and utensils are displayed in an area called the Treasury. Icons, painted by the abbot, are also for sale.

✚ 116 C3 ✉ 3km (2 miles) south of (Pano) Panagia ☎ 2672 2457

🕐 Daily 9–sunset. Treasury: closed 12.30–1.30 🖐 Free. Treasury: inexpensive 🍴 Café outside monastery (£)

GEROSKIPOU

The church of Agia Paraskevi, in the centre of the village, is famous throughout the island because of its distinctive five-domed plan. The building itself dates from the 10th-century but it has a number of decorations over the altar that date from the 9th century. The paintings are slightly later, and are believed to be from the 12th to the 15th century.

There is also an excellent Folk Art Museum, just off the main street, which contains farming and domestic implements as well as traditional costumes. The village is known for its *Loukoumi* ('Cyprus delight', called 'Turkish delight' before the Turkish invasion); it is possible to watch it being made in some of the shops and there are plenty of opportunities to buy some.

✚ 116 E2 ✉ 3km (2 miles) east of Pafos ☎ Agia Paraskevi: 2696 1859. Art Museum: 2630 6216 🕐 Church: Apr–Oct Mon–Sat 8–1, 2–5; Nov–Mar Mon–Sat 8–1, 2–4, Sun 10–1. Folk Art Museum: Mon–Wed, Fri 9–2.30, Thu 9–2.30, 3–5. Closed afternoons Jul–Aug 🖐 Church: free. Folk Art Museum: inexpensive 🚌 From Pafos old town

LARA

See pages 30–31.

PALAIA PAFOS (OLD PAFOS)/KOUKLIA

The site, on which stands the Sanctuary of Aphrodite, is spread
over a large area. At the entrance is a restored Lusignan manor (La
Covocle) with substantial and impressive Turkish additions. In its
main hall is a museum with exhibits focusing on the history of the
excavation of the area and the fragments of mosaic that have
been found. Its prize possession is a large black stone that stood
as a manifestation of Aphrodite and was worshipped by pilgrims.
The hall itself is worth a closer look as it is one of the best
examples of 13th-century Gothic architecture on the island.

To the east of the museum are Roman remains, including
remnants of the Sanctuary of Aphrodite, which stands around a
courtyard where rituals took place. The south wing is the best
preserved, and parts of the original walls still stand.

West of the sanctuary are the ruins of Roman houses, including the House of Leda; follow the path that leads to a replica of a mosaic of Leda and the Swan.

➕ 116 E3 ✉ 14km (8.5 miles) east of Pafos ☎ 2643 2180 🕓 Daily 9–4. Closed 1 Jan, 25 Dec, Greek Orthodox Easter Sun ✋ Museum: inexpensive. Rest of the site: free

PANAGIA

The village of (Pano) Panagia is the place where Archbishop Makarios was born. Makarios played a key role in the campaign for independence from the British and he was the first president of Cyprus from independence in 1960 until his death in 1977.

His parents' house in the village is now a museum. It consists of two rooms, with his parents' bed, assorted crockery and family photographs. If nothing else, the house shows that Archbishop Makarios had a humble background. In the main square is a cultural centre, which displays more photographs and memorabilia from his later life as president.

➕ 116 C4 ✉ (Pano) Panagia village centre 🕓 Cultural Centre: May–Sep daily 9–1, 3–6; Oct–Apr daily 9–1, 2–4. Makarios's House: daily 9–2, 2–4 ✋ Cultural Centre: free. Makarios's House: donation requested 🍴 Many cafés in village (£)

POLIS

The town has traditionally been a destination for backpackers and other more unconventional travellers. Most of the main restaurants and shops are found around a pedestrianised square, with a number of rooms and apartments to rent close by. There is a good beach a short walk from the town centre, with a campsite adjacent.

Just east of the town, but difficult to identify, is the ancient site of Marion, which was founded in the 7th century BC and developed into one of the 10 city kingdoms of Cyprus.

✚ 116 B2

POMOS

There are some wonderful quiet beaches along this section of coast, and as the road climbs up into the cliffs there are amazing views. Just beyond Pomos Point is a small fishing harbour and sheltered beach. Kokkina is occupied by the Turkish army and is inaccessible. The road detours inland and then reaches Kato Pyrgos where there is another isolated beach.

✚ 116 A3 ✉ 22km (13.5 miles) northwest of Polis 🍴 Cafés at Kato Pyrgos (£) 🚌 Limited bus service from Polis to Pomos, at 11, 2, 4, 6; Sat 11, 2.30, 4

Nicosia and The High Troodos

Nicosia (Lefkosia) lies inland on the Mesaoria, or central plain. This location allowed the city to avoid the devastation wreaked on the coastal towns by Arab raiders. Here the plain is relatively narrow, with the Pentadaktylos Mountains to the north and the foothills of the Troodos approaching the city from the southwest.

The northern boundary is no arbitrary choice: the Green Line that still divides Cyprus cuts through the heart of Nicosia. But visitors will now find it a frontier they can cross at several points in Nicosia as well as elsewhere along its length.

To the south is a splendid area of valleys and villages; Stavros tis Psokas in the west is a lonely forest station; Machairas Monastery and its surrounding hills make up the eastern extremity.

Nicosia (Lefkosia)

NICOSIA

Despite the opening of the border, Nicosia, the capital of Cyprus, remains a divided city. The border, known as the Green Line, separates the Greek Cypriot and Turkish Cypriot parts of the island and runs through the middle of the city. The Greek Cypriot side has all the hallmarks of a modern westernized place and is a thriving shopping and business centre, though its ancient history is visible. The Turkish Cypriot sector has a more dilapidated and Eastern feel, with narrower streets and old-fashioned shops.

Nicosia is always busy and is always hotter than the coast, so summer visitors should not plan too strenuous a programme. Fortunately the main attractions are within the old city walls and can be explored on foot. The walls themselves, built by the Venetians, still impress.

An extensive modernization and refurbishment programme is underway in the old part of town. The traffic-free Laïki Geitonia area is the most obvious result of that programme; it is a pleasant place to wander, with all the facilities a tourist could need, and leads into some of the older shopping streets.

There is less to see in northern Nicosia and the narrow streets make it easy to get lost. However, almost all roads eventually lead to the main sight, the Selimiye Mosque, once the Cathedral of Santa Sophia, the minarets of which dominate this part of town.

There are a number of other mosques in the vicinity, plus a few small museums and, for the more adventurous, the Turkish Baths.

✚ 118 A3

Greek Cypriot Nicosia

AGIOS IOANNIS CATHEDRAL

The cathedral lies within the episcopal precinct and was built in 1662 on the site of a Benedictine abbey church. It contains some fine 18th-century wall paintings and is ornately decorated throughout. It is claimed that it contained the finger of St John the Baptist until it was stolen by Mameluke raiders. The cathedral is smaller than one might expect of a building of importance and is best visited early.

➕ 126 C3 ✉ Plateia Archiepiskopou Kyprianou ⏰ Mon–Fri 8–12, 2–4, Sat 8–12 ✋ Free 🍴 Cafés nearby (£)

ARCHBISHOP MAKARIOS CULTURAL CENTRE (BYZANTINE MUSEUM)

The most important exhibits in the museum are the 6th-century Kanakaria Mosaics, which were thought lost when they were stolen from their church on the Karpasia peninsula in northern Cyprus. They were recovered when offered for sale on the international art market and were returned to this purpose-built wing of the museum. Also on show are a large number of icons from churches around the island.

➕ 126 C3 ✉ Plateia Archiepiskopou Kyprianou ☎ 2243 0008 🕐 Mon–Fri 9–4.30, Sat 9–1 💵 Moderate 🍴 Cafés nearby (£)

CYPRUS MUSEUM

The museum houses most of the important finds from sites across Cyprus – neolithic artefacts, Bronze Age vases and clay figurines, Mycenaean objects from Kourion (➤ 26–27) and sophisticated pottery. Two thousand figurines found at Agia Irini are displayed as they were found, gathered around a single altar. A wide range of sculptures are on show, as well as a huge bronze statue of Roman Emperor Septimius Severus and the famous horned god from Enkomi. There are impressive items from Salamis (➤ 38–39), some mosaics and a reconstructed rock-cut tomb.

➕ 126 C1 ✉ Leoforos Mouseiou ☎ 2286 5888 🕐 Mon–Sat 9–5, Sun 10–1. Closed 1 Jan, 25 Dec, Greek Orthodox Easter Sun 💵 Moderate 🍴 Café opposite (££)

FAMAGUSTA GATE

This was the main entrance into the old city from the south and east. It is set into the historic walls and has been restored to house a cultural centre that is used for exhibitions and other events. Artists have set up studios in old buildings in the area.

126 C4 ⊠ Leoforos Athinon ☎ 2243 0877 ⏲ Mon–Fri 10–1, 4–7, (5–8 Jun–Aug) ✋ Free 🍴 Cafés nearby (£)

HADJIGEORGAKIS KORNESIOS HOUSE (ETHNOGRAPHICAL MUSEUM)

This house belonged to the grand dragoman of Cyprus, Hadjigeorgakis Kornesios, at the end of the 18th century. The dragoman was an interlocutor between the ethnic Greek and Turkish populations, an important and powerful role at that time. The museum contains a number of artefacts from the dragoman's life, displayed in reconstructions of some of the original rooms, along with letters and documents prepared by Kornesios.

126 C3 ⊠ Odos Patriarchou Grigoriou ☎ 2230 5316 ⏲ Mon–Fri 9–5.30 ✋ Inexpensive 🍴 Cafés nearby (£)

LAÏKI GEITONIA

This is a revived traffic-free area of old Nicosia where traditional buildings have been restored, shops refurbished and trees planted. It is specifically aimed at the tourist, with a whole range of restaurants, craft shops and the tourist office, as well as a small jewellery museum.

The old shopping streets of Lidras and Onasagoras that lead out of the Laïki Geitonia area are also interesting places to wander. Rather more traditional shops are found on these streets and at their northern end are the sandbags that mark the Green Line.

✚ 126 C2 ✉ Within old city walls, northeast of Plateia Eleftherias 🍴 Many cafés (££)

LEVENTIS MUNICIPAL MUSEUM OF NICOSIA

This museum, in Laïki Geitonia, is well set out and modest in size. Medieval finds, some of which were uncovered when the building was being restored, are in the basement. The first floor deals with the period 2300BC to the Turkish era and the ground floor covers the British colonial time as well as the city's recent history. The documentation from this later time is particularly interesting although the commentaries can be a little partisan.

✚ 126 C2 ✉ Odos Ippokratou ☎ 2266 1475 🕐 Tue–Sun 10–4.30. Closed 1 Jan, 25 Dec, Greek Orthodox Easter Sun ♨ Free 🍴 Café in basement (££)

OMERIYE MOSQUE

As with many of the city's mosques, this building was originally a church, converted in 1571 by Lala Mustafa Paşa, the occupying Turkish general. He believed that the visit of the Muslim prophet Omar should be commemorated, and as a result the minaret was added and the old Lusignan tombstones used to cover the floor. The mosque is still used as a place of worship.

✚ 126 C3 ✉ Odos Trikoupi 🕐 Any reasonable hour and when there is prayer ♨ Free, donation expected 🍴 Cafés nearby (£)

Turkish Cypriot Nicosia (Lefkoşa)

BÜYÜK HAMAM

This was once the Church of St George, built in the 14th century and subsequently converted to a bathhouse by the Turks. The main room is domed, the floor well below street level. On Fridays only women are permitted inside, other days men only. Should it be locked, the café owner on the west side has the key.

✚ 126 B2 ✉ Mousa Orfenbey Sokağı 🕐 Jun–Sep daily 7.30–1, 4–6; Oct–May daily 8–1, 2–6 ✋ Free entry. Baths: moderate 🍴 Café next door (£)

BÜYÜK HAN

The building was commissioned in 1572 by Lala Mustafa Paşa, the

first Ottoman governor of Cyprus. It was a simple inn, complete with stables and a wonderful little mosque in the courtyard. Perhaps the nadir of its fortunes was when it became Nicosia's central prison in 1893. Its days of neglect are now over – the Department of Antiquities has restored it, albeit as a museum, and it now houses small shops and cafés, as well as serving as a venue for occasional concerts.

✚ 126 B2 ✉ Arasta Sokağı 🕐 Mon, Wed–Thu 8–8, Tue and Fri 8–midnight, Sat 8–3 ✋ Inexpensive

LAPIDARY MUSEUM

The building, on two levels, was perhaps once the home of a wealthy Venetian family. Assorted wooden relics from mosques and churches display fine carving. In the courtyard is a random selection of Corinthian capitals, carved stone heads and a section of a beautiful rose window.

✠ 126 B3 ✉ Northeast of the Selimiye Mosque 🕐 Jun–Sep daily 9–2; Oct–May 9–1, 2–2.45. If locked, try custodian at the Library of Sultan Mahmut II across the road 💰 Inexpensive

MEVLEVI TEKKE (ETHNOGRAPHICAL MUSEUM)

This was the home of the whirling dervishes, a sect founded in the 13th century. The rooms have a simple elegance, complete with a splendid minstrels' gallery looking down on where the dervishes, heads lowered in contemplation, would stretch out their arms and spin at ever increasing speed. In 1925 Kemal Atatürk forbade such dancing in an attempt to modernize Turkish culture. After 20 years the ruling was relaxed and the dance celebrated once more. To one side is a collection of costumes, wedding dresses and musical instruments.

➕ 126 A2 ✉ Girne Caddesi 🕓 Jun–Sep Mon–Fri 9–2; Oct–Mar daily 9–1, 2–4.45 ✋ Moderate

SELIMIYE MOSQUE

This impressive building was a Christian masterpiece before conversion to a mosque of the Ottoman Turks, the most important in Cyprus. The elevations of magnificent windows, portals and buttresses are discordant; the reason – the soaring minarets. They are landmarks in the walled city, and their imposition on the west front by the Turks reflects the momentous events of 1570–71.

The original cathedral was started in 1209 and substantially completed 117 years later. In reality it was never quite finished, work carrying on long after the consecration.

Everything changed with the arrival of the Turks. All the overt Christian decoration of the cathedral was destroyed. Soon work was started on the minarets and the building became the Cathedral of Santa Sophia until the name was changed to the Selimiye Mosque in 1954.

➕ 126 B3 ✉ Selimiye Sokağı 🕓 Daily ✋ Free

What to See in the High Troodos

AGIOS IRAKLEIDIOS

The monastery was founded in the Byzantine era, and it is dedicated to the saint who guided St Paul and St Barnabas to nearby Tamassos during their missionary travels. St Irakleidios lived in a cave, and the first church was built around it. His skull is kept in the present building in a silver reliquary, and many believe it has miraculous powers to heal the sick.

The complex is now a convent. It dates from 1773 and is a simple construction of good appearance, with excellent gardens. These are meticulously tended by the nuns and in summer are an oasis of greenery and colour in the barren landscape.

➕ 117 B8 ✉ Near the village of Politikon ⌚ Group visits only: Mon, Tue, Thu 9–12 ✋ Free 🍴 Café opposite (£)

ASINOU CHURCH (PANAGIA FORVIOTISSA)

The fame of this church is such that it is quite a surprise to find it so tiny, hidden on a north-facing hillside of eucalyptus and pine trees. A steep clay-tiled outer roof protects the vulnerable Byzantine dome and treasures within.

Asinou remains unscathed after 900 years. The frescoes are the best of Cyprus's painted churches, the earliest dating back to the 12th century. They were added to over the years and culminate in the powerful work by refugee painters from Asia Minor.

Christ is depicted in the sanctuary and the dome of the narthex, gazing down. All around, the rank and file are beautifully illustrated.

➕ 117 B6 ✉ Near Nikitari ⌚ Summer daily 9–5; winter 9–4; ask in Nikitari for the priest with the key ✋ Free

KAKOPETRIA

This village stands high in the poplar-lined Solea Valley. As hill villages go, it is quite large and is a popular holiday resort of Cypriots. It is certainly not a smart place, the buildings are generally old or ramshackle or both, but it has charm and many traditional dwellings are being restored.

Up the valley (3km/2 miles) is the celebrated church of **Agios Nikolaos tis Stegis** with its famous roof. Below the town, at Galata, are the tiny churches of Panagia Eleousa and Panagia Theotokos, looking like country barns, with their roofs nearly touching the ground.

✚ 117 C6

Agios Nikolaos tis Stegis

⏰ Tue–Sat 9–4, Sun 11–4 ✋ Free 🍴 Several cafés (£–££)

KYKKOS MONASTERY

See pages 28–29.

MACHAIRAS MONASTERY

The monastery was founded in the 12th century and grew around
an icon of the Virgin Mary. Successive fires destroyed the original
church and its wall paintings and in 1892 the entire monastery was
burned to the ground.

The present building dates from the early 20th century, and its
elevations are fortress-like, broken up with wooden balconies.
Within is an impressive iconostasis, illuminated by chandeliers.
On feast days rituals take place starting early and culminating
at midnight with the abbot emerging with the holy fire, a
glowing candle.

Outside a track leads down the wooded valley to the cave of
Grigoris Afxentiou, second in command of EOKA during the
uprising against the British. In 1957 a shepherd betrayed him and

British soldiers surrounded the cave entrance. Afxentiou chose to fight, dying eight hours later in his hideout.

✚ 117 C8 ✉ Near Fikardou, eastern Troodos ◷ Group visits only: Mon, Tue, Thu 9–12 ✋ Free 🍴 Cafés nearby (£)

MOUNT OLYMPOS

At 1,951m (6,399ft) above sea level, the summit of Mount Olympos is the highest ground in Cyprus. It is not an inaccessible peak, as a narrow road winds towards the top, stopping just below the summit at an unappealing radar dome and other military facilities. As a mountain it is thereby compromised. with no chance of proceeding higher to experience the view. This is reserved for those on the other, more inaccessible, side of the hill. In winter it is an unforgettable experience to stand in deep snow, bathed in sunlight, and look over to Morfou Bay and the Taurus Mountains of Turkey beyond.

✚ 117 C5 ✉ 55km (34 miles) from Limassol, 97km (60 miles) from Nicosia 🍴 Cafés in Troodos village 4km (2.5 miles) away (£)

PANAGIA TOU ARAKA

The paintings in this church are marvellous. Unfortunately the drive to get there is long and tiring, albeit through superb scenery. Should the church be locked, admission is then by courtesy of the priest, normally found in the village of Lagoudera.

The church retains the most complete series of wall paintings of the Byzantine period on the island and they have been restored, courtesy of UNESCO. They represent the metropolitan classicizing school in full bloom. Even visitors who know little of this Byzantine style will surely appreciate their magnificence.

✚ 117 C6 ✉ Lagoudera ⏱ Daily 10–4 ✋ Free 🍴 Café in nearby village (£)

The North

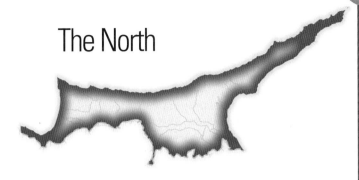

This is the Turkish-controlled part of Cyprus, underpopulated compared to the remainder of the island. Change has been slow in coming, perhaps

due to the easy-going temperament of the Turkish Cypriots, but since the opening of the border in 2003 the pace has been steadily picking up.

Whatever the objectives of trade embargoes on this area they cannot detract from the magnificent scenery, and they have, to a diminishing extent, held back destructive mass tourism.

Along the north shore the spectacular Pentadaktylos (Beşparmak) Mountains run unbroken for 90km (56 miles). To the south the land is flat, opening out into the Mesaoria east of Nicosia. In summer it is impressively barren: in spring the colour has to be seen to be believed.

The narrow Karpasia peninsula is spectacular, with the blue Mediterranean visible to north and south.

Famagusta (Gazimağusa)

The city is divided, although not between Greek Cypriot and Turkish Cypriot. Varosha, the new town, with its painted hotels bordering the sandy beach, is closed to all but the military, as it has been since 1974. Visitors concentrate on the walled city. They are adequately compensated in that it is one of the finest surviving examples of medieval military architecture.

To pass through the massive walls is to pass through history, from the time of the Lusignans, Genoese and Venetians to the bloody siege by the Turks in 1570–71. They stormed the walls and all Cyprus was theirs for over 300 years.

In the narrow streets shops are unchanged by time or fashion. Dark interiors hide a miscellany of goods. The town can be a bustling place of noise and activity, but more often it is calm. They may not be as outgoing as their Greek Cypriot countrymen in the south, but Turkish Cypriots are equally courteous and helpful.

There is much unexpected open space in all directions: a chaotic panorama of unkempt gardens and scrubland, where palm trees shade ancient domed churches. Crumbling medieval buildings are all around. The battered minaret and massive buttress of Lala Mustafa Paşa Mosque form an impressive landmark.

✚ 122 F3

LALA MUSTAFA PAŞA MOSQUE

The building has been a mosque for over 400 years, but, the architecture is of a Gothic cathedral. There is a single minaret, well executed but certainly out of place. Even so, you can still admire the splendid six-light window of the west front. Three portals lead to the impressive interior, where Moslem simplicity has allowed the fine nave to survive the loss of its Christian decoration.

Lala Mustafa was the victorious commander of the Ottoman Turks when they broke into Famagusta in 1571. Surprisingly, the

mosque only received his name in 1954, before which it was
called the Mosque of Santa Sophia.

🖂 Naim Efendi Sokağı ⏰ Daily 💷 Free 🍴 Café opposite west front (£)

ST GEORGE OF THE GREEKS

This is a substantial church, though it has deteriorated significantly
(it was built in 1359). The three apses are semicircular. A dome
covered the middle section of the church, but by all accounts it
collapsed under cannon fire in 1571. Some wall paintings survive,
the best being in the eastern apse.

🖂 Mustafa Ersu Sokağı ⏰ Daily 💷 Free

ST PETER AND ST PAUL (SINAN PAŞA MOSQUE)

This Gothic church is distinctive for its spectacular flying buttresses. It was subsequently used as a mosque, as the ruined minaret in one corner testifies, and has also served as the municipal library. At other times it stored potatoes and grain and was known as the wheat mosque. On entering, the reason for the massive buttresses is apparent – the nave is of tremendous height, exerting a colossal force on the outside walls.

✉ Abdullah Paşa Sokağı 🕐 Jun–Sep Mon–Fri 9–2; Oct–May Mon–Fri 9–1, 2–4.45 ✋ Inexpensive 🍴 Cafés nearby (£)

VENETIAN WALLS

The original plan of the town was laid out by the Lusignans, but, when the Venetians took over in 1489 they completely renovated the enclosing walls. Experts in military architecture, they lowered the walls but increased the thickness, taking out all features that were vulnerable to cannon fire.

Any tour of the fortifications should take into account the great heat of summer and the low parapets everywhere.

The Citadel should be visited. It is also known as Othello's Tower, a name derived from Shakespeare's play, set in 'Cyprus. A seaport' and 'Cyprus. The Citadel'. Four great cylindrical towers guard the corners of the Citadel, and the carving over the entrance is an impressive winged lion of St Mark. The great hall is a massive vaulted chamber.

Taking a clockwise circuit of the walls, the Sea Gate, 200m (218yds) southeast, is the next place of interest. The gate's portcullis is part of the original Venetian work. In another 500m (545yds) is the Canbulat Gate and bastion (Canbulat was a Turkish hero of the siege), now a museum. Muskets and swords are displayed next to period dresses finished with fine embroidery.

Three bastions on the south wall lead to the Land Gate, the main entrance to the town. It is part of the Ravelin, a bastion considered impregnable when built, but later found wanting as its ditch offered cover to the enemy.

🕐 Citadel and Museum: Jun–Sep daily 9–7; Oct–May 9–1, 2–4.45 ✋ Citadel: moderate. Museum: inexpensive 🍴 Cafés nearby (£)

What to See in The North

BELAPAIS ABBEY

The setting of the abbey on the northern slopes of the Pentadaktylos (Beşparmak) Mountains is marvellous. Far below are almond and olive groves on the coastal plain, and Keryneia (Girne) seen to the west. Augustinian canons founded the abbey at the end of the 12th century, its importance lasting for some 300 years. Substantial parts collapsed long ago. The cloister is half ruined and flamboyant tracery hangs down from the pointed arches. On the north side

is the refectory, where the vault appears to spring lightly from the supporting capitals. Six tall windows look out on to the northern shore, and there is an exquisite pulpit, reached by an intricate stair constructed in the thickness of the wall. The 13th-century church is generally locked, but the custodian may open it on request.

In 1995 forest fires swept through the Pentadaktylos Mountains, advancing rapidly on Belapais (Beylerbeyi), the village where the author Lawrence Durrell lived from 1953 to 1956. In his celebrated *Bitter Lemons* he had written 'two things spread quickly; gossip and a forest fire'. It was only good fortune and the skill of the firefighters that prevented the destruction of Beylerbeyi in July 1995.

➕ 120 C4 ✉ Belapais (Beylerbeyi) village ◷ Jun–Sep daily 9–7; Oct–May daily 9–1, 2–4.45 ✋ Moderate 🍴 Café at the gate (£)

KANTARA

Kantara is the most easterly of the great Lusignan fortresses of the northern shore. At 600m (1,968ft) above sea level, its walls crown rocky crags, with the north shore way below.

The location at the eastern end of the Pentadaktylos (Beşparmak) Mountains gave the garrison control of the Karpasia peninsula. Visitors can, in a brief panorama, survey this unique landscape in its entirety.

Most of the castle is a ruin, although the formidable outer wall is substantially intact. Entrance is gained through a ruined barbican and two towers. Steps lead on to vaulted chambers and medieval latrines. On the highest ground, only a Gothic window remains.

🚩 122 C3 ⊠ Near Kantara village ⏱ Jun–Sep daily 10–5; Oct–May daily 9–1, 2–4.45 ✋ Moderate 🍴 Cafés in Kantara village (£)

KERYNEIA (GIRNE)

Keryneia is unmatched in the rest of Cyprus. This is all to do with the harbour and its magnificent setting. Certainly the old buildings of the quayside, with the exception of the customs houses, have all been reconstituted as restaurants and bars, nevertheless everything seems just perfect, day or night.

A huge cylindrical bastion from Venetian times forms the east end of the harbour, a minaret rises up in the middle ground and the bell-tower of the former Archangelos Michaïl church, now an icon museum, is in the west. Mountain ridges and summits run unbroken into the hazy distance.

The origins of the **castle** are Lusignan, but it was the Venetians who made it impregnable (and then surrendered it to the Turks without a fight in 1570). Inside, sunlight streams down from hidden windows and openings. Entry into the complex structure is over the moat, now dry, to reach a gatehouse. Progress is then up a ramp, passing a small Byzantine chapel and continuing to the northwest tower, where there is the tomb of Sadık Paşa, killed in 1570. Various routes can be taken to complete a tour of the castle, but care is needed to keep clear of the unguarded drops.

The shipwreck museum within the castle is a highlight. It houses the remains of a Hellenistic-era merchant ship, raised from the seabed between 1968 and 1969. The blackened hull, astonishingly well preserved, is more than 2,300 years old.

✚ 120 C4 🍴 Cafés around the harbour (£–££)

Keryneia Castle

✉ Harbour ⏱ Jun–Sep daily 9–7; Oct–May daily 9–1, 2–4.45 👋 Expensive

ST HILARION CASTLE
See pages 36–37.

SALAMIS
See pages 38–39.

SOLOI (SOLI)
The founders of Soli came from Greece and they created a city destined to play a major role in the struggle against Persian rule in the 5th and 4th centuries BC. However, only the later work of the Romans survives. They cut a theatre out of a rocky hillside overlooking Morfou Bay; today, most of this substantial work is a reconstruction. Near the road are the remains of a colonnade leading to an agora. Some mosaics remain, the bird representations being most impressive.

The wealth of Soli lay with its copper, mined from the surrounding hills. Boats from the city's harbour, long silted up, carried the metal to various parts of the Mediterranean.

✚ 117 A5 ✉ Near Gemikonağı ⏰ Jun–Sep daily 9–7; Oct–May daily 9–1, 2–4.45 💲 Moderate

VOUNI

The road to ruined Vouni Palace spirals spectacularly upwards, a splendid area where the Troodos Mountains meet the northern shore. A series of terraces, swept bare by time, climb the hillside.

The palace was clearly a substantial construction, with apartments, baths and courtyards. It was built in the 5th century BC by a pro-Persian king from Marion, possibly to counter the power of nearby Soli, a city loyal to the Greeks.

The baths have a water system comparable to those of the Romans, but it is centuries earlier. At the top of the hill are the ruins of the Greek-style Temple of Athena.

🚩 117 A5 ✉ Near Gemikonağı ⏱ Jun–Sep daily 10–5; Oct–May daily 9–1, 2–4.45 💲 Moderate

Index

Acknowledgements

The Automobile Association would like to thank the following photographers, companies and picture libraries for their assistance in the preparation of this book.

Abbreviations for the picture credits are as follows: - (t) top; (b) bottom; (l) left; (r) right; (AA) AA World Travel Library.

4l Larnaka Airport, AA/A Kouprianoff; **4c** Kyrenia, AA/A Kouprianoff; **4r** Lefkara, AA/S Day; **5l** Pano, AA/R Rainford; **5r** Petra tou Romiou, AA/M Birkitt; **6/7** Larnaka Airport, AA/A Kouprianoff; **10** Greek dancers, AA/M Birkitt; **12** Motorbike and car rental, AA/M Birkitt; **13** Signpost, AA/A Kouprianoff; **14** Tour bus, AA/A Kouprianoff; **15** Taxi driver, AA/A Kouprianoff; **16** Public telephone, AA/M Birkitt; **20/21** Kyrenia, AA/A Kouprianoff; **22** Akamas Peninsular, AA/S Day; **22/23** Akamas Peninsular, AA/S Day; **23** Walkers, Akamas Peninsular, AA/S Day; **24** Embroidery, Mevlevi Tekke, AA/M Birkitt; **24/25** Salt Lake, AA/A Kouprianoff; **25** Hala Sultan Tekke Mosque, AA/S Day; **26** Column, Kourion, AA/M Birkitt; **26/27** Ruins of Kourion, AA/R Rainford; **27** Amphitheatre, Kourion, AA/M Birkitt; **28/29** Kykkos Monastery, AA/S Day; **29** Kykkos Monastery, AA/A Kouprianoff; **30** Petrol tank, AA/R Rainford; **30/31** Cape Lara, AA/S Day; **31t** Turtles, Lara beach, AA/A Kouprianoff; **31b** Turtle, Lara beach, AA/A Kouprianoff; **32/33** Venetian walls, Nicosia, AA/S Day; **33t** Venetian walls, Nicosia, AA/A Kouprianoff; **33b** Cyclist, Laiki Geitonia, AA/S Day; **34t** Mosaic, Pafos, AA/R Rainford; **34b** Tomb of the Kings, Pafos, AA/M Birkitt; **34/35** Mosaic, Pafos, AA/A Kouprianoff; **36** St Hilarion Castle, AA/A Kouprianoff; **36/37** St Hilarion Castle, AA/A Kouprianoff; **38** City of Salamis, AA/A Kouprianoff; **38/39** Colonnades, City of Salamis, AA/A Kouprianoff; **39** Kampanopetra Basilica, Salamis, AA/A Kouprianoff; **40** Tilliria, Troodos, AA/A Kouprianoff; **40/41** Kaledonia Falls, Troodos, AA/A Kouprianoff; **41** Fruit seller, AA/M Birkitt; **42/43** Lefkara, AA/S Day; **45** Priest, AA/S Day; **46** Agios Lazaros, Larnaka, AA/A Kouprianoff; **46/47** Larnaka, AA/M Birkitt; **48/49** Ruins, Kition, AA/M Birkitt; **49t** Pierides Foundation Museum, Larnaka, AA/A Kouprianoff; **49b** Cannon, Larnaka, AA/M Birkitt; **50** Harbour, Agia Napa, AA/M Birkitt; **51** Tekke of Hala Sultan, AA/A Kouprianoff; **52** Nissi Bay, AA/R Rainford; **52/53** Potamos Harbour, AA/S Day; **54/55** Stavrovouni Monastry, AA/R Rainford; **56** Fishing nets, AA/A Kouprianoff; **57** Restaurant, Limassol, AA/M Birkitt; **59** Beachside café, Limassol, AA/M Birkitt; **60/61** Artillery fortress, Limassol, AA/M Birkitt; **61** Cyprus Museum, Nicosia, AA/R Rainford; **62/63** Zoo gardens, Limassol, AA/M Birkitt; **63** Salt Lake, AA/A Kouprianoff; **64** Khirokitia Neolitic village, AA/M Birkitt; **65** Kolossi Castle, AA/A Kouprianoff; **66** Café, Lefkara, AA/S Day; **66/67** Rock of Aphrodite, AA/S Day; **68** Sanctuary of Apollo Hylates, AA/A Kouprianoff; **69** Pafos harbour, AA/M Birkitt; **70/71** Catacomb, Pafos, AA/A Kouprianoff; **72/73** Harbour, Pafos, AA/M Birkitt; **73** St Paul's Pillar, Pafos, AA/S Day; **74** Saranda Kolones, AA/S Day; **75** Tomb of the Kings, Pafos, AA/M Birkitt; **76/77** Agios Neofytos Monastery, AA/S Day; **78/79** Panagia Chrysorrogiatissa Monastery, AA/A Kouprianoff; **79** Ayia Paraskevi, Geroskipou, AA/S Day; **80/81** Palaia Pafos Museum, AA/M Birkitt; **81** Archbishop Makarios house-museum, AA/M Birkitt; **82** Church, Polis, AA/A Kouprianoff; **82/83** Coastline, Pomos, AA/A Kouprianoff; **84** Lace-maker, AA/A Kouprianoff; **85** Market trader, AA/R Rainford; **86** Archbishop Makarios statue, AA/S Day; **86/87** Agios Ioannis cathedral, AA/A Kouprianoff; **87** Agios Ioannis cathedral, AA/M Birkitt; **88** Cyprus Museum, Nicosia, AA/R Rainford; **88/89** Cyprus Museum, Nicosia, AA/A Kouprianoff; **89** Famagusta Gate, Nicosia, AA/M Birkitt; **90** Omeriye Mosque, AA/M Birkitt; **92** Mosque, Buyuk Han, AA/R Bulmar; **92/93** Buyuk Han, AA/M Birkitt; **93** Turkish Cypriot lady, AA/M Birkitt; **94** Museum of Folk Art, AA/A Kouprianoff; **95** Selimiye Mosque, AA/A Kouprianoff; **96/97** Kakopetria, AA/M Birkitt; **98/99** Machairas Monastery, AA/M Birkitt; **99** Artemis trail, AA/A Kouprianoff; **100** Byzantine monastery, AA/A Kouprianoff; **101** Famagusta, AA/A Kouprianoff; **103** Lala Mustafa Pasa Mosque, AA/A Kouprianoff; **104** Sinan Pasa Camii, AA/A Kouprianoff; **104/105** Venetian walls, Famagusta, AA/H Ulucam; **106** Belapais Abbey, AA/A Kouprianoff; **107** Kantara Castle, AA/R Bulmar; **108/109** Kyrenia harbour, AA; **110** Theatre, Soloi, AA/H Ulucam; **111t** Ruins, Soloi, AA; **111b** Streetscene, Vouni, AA/A Kouprianoff.

Every effort has been made to trace the copyright holders, and we apologise in advance for any accidental errors. We would be happy to apply the corrections in the following edition of this publication.

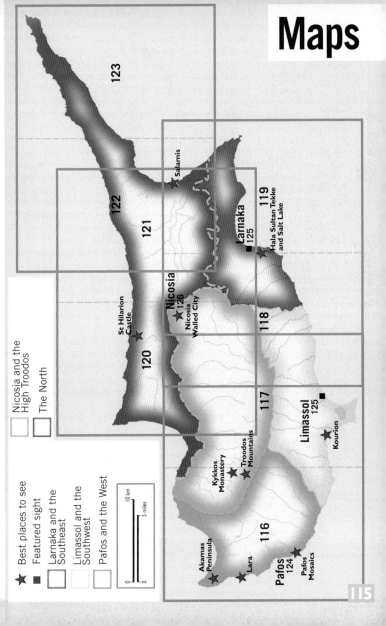

Maps

Best places to see ★
Featured sight ■

Nicosia and the High Troodos
The North
Larnaka and the Southeast
Limassol and the Southwest
Pafos and the West

123

122
121

120

Salamis ★

St Hilarion Castle ★

Nicosia 126
★ Nicosia Walled City

118

Larnaka 125 ■
★ Hala Sultan Tekke and Salt Lake

119

117

Limassol 125 ■
Kourion ★

Kykkos Monastery ★
★ Troodos Mountains

Akamas Peninsula ★
Lara ★

116

Pafos 124
★ Pafos Mosaics

10 km
5 miles

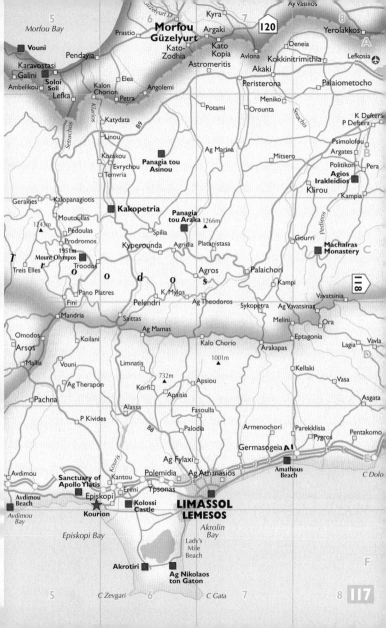

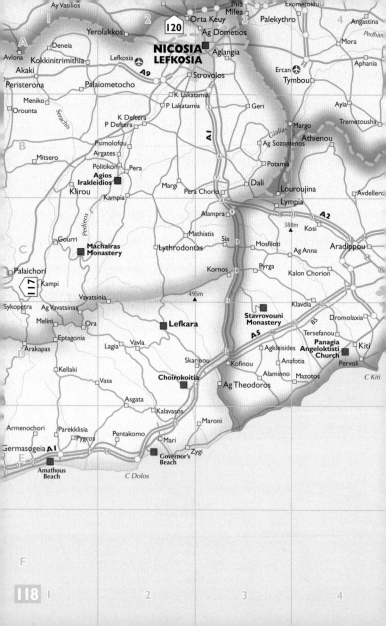

A

B

C

1 2 3 4

D

E

F

Ephtakomi

Kantara ■

□ Komi Kebir

□ Kantara

Akanthou
□

Ovgoros
□
Yerani
□

Patriki □

□ Ay Theodo

▲ 740m

Mandres □

Topsiou
Keuy □

Ardhana
□

□ Gastria

Ay. Amvrosios
□
□ Kalogrea

Meloúnda
□

□ Platani

□ Ay. Iakovos

Boghaz

C E

□ Kharcha

□ Trypimeni

Ay. Khariton □

Gouphes
□

Lapathos
□

Trikomo
□

Kornokipos
□

Knodhara
□

Lefkoniko
□

Gypsos
□

Syngrasis
□

Kalyvakia □
Chatos □

Psilatos
□

Milia
□

Spathariko
□

Famagusta Bay

Marathovouno
□

Yenagra
□

Piyi
□

Sandalaris
□

Angastina
□

Kanli D

★ Salamis

Pedhieos

Cakilli

Mora □

Prastio
□

Asha
□

Sinda
□

Styllos
□

Gaidhouras
□

Engomi
□

Aphania
□

**FAMAGUSTA
(GAZIMAGUSA)** ■

Vatili
□

Akhyritou
□

Ayia □

Lysi
□

Kondea
□

Kalopsidha
□

Tremetousha □

□ Arsos

Makrasyka
□

119

Akhna □

2 3 4

Deryneia ■

Frenaros

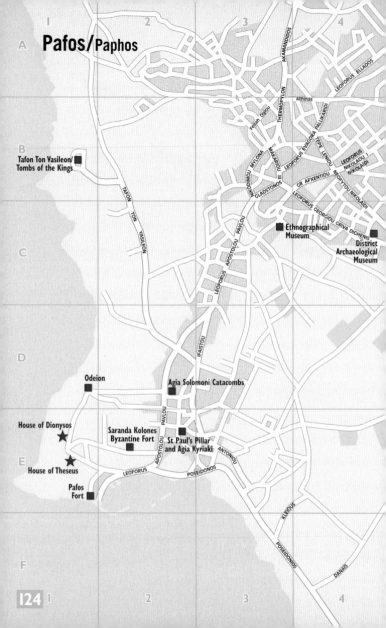

Pafos/Paphos

A

B

**Tafon Ton Vasileon/
Tombs of the Kings**

C

**Ethnographical
Museum**

**District
Archaeological
Museum**

D

Odeion

Agia Solomoni Catacombs

E

House of Dionysos

**Saranda Kolones
Byzantine Fort**

**St Paul's Pillar
and Agia Kyriaki**

House of Theseus

**Pafos
Fort**

F

124

Nicosia/
Lefkosia

OSMAN PASA CADD
CEMAL GÜRSEL CADD
KARAOĞLANOĞLU
İstanbul Şok
M. Akıncı Şok

Mevlevi
Tekke

Büyük Hamam

Lapidary
Museum

Büyük Han

Selimiye
Mosque

Walled
City

Famagusta Gate

Archbishop Makarios
Cultural Centre

Agios Ioannis Theologos

Cyprus
Museum

Omeriye
Museum

Hadjigeorgakis
Kornesios House

Leventis
Municipal
Museum

Laiki Geitonia

LEOFORUS MARKOU DRAKOU
SEPT
KINYRA
LEOFORUS AVGYPTOU
RIGENIS
OMIROU
METOCHIOU
CHILONOS
L K PANTELIDI
ONASAGOROU
LIDRAS
TRIKOUPI
PALAIOLOGOU
LEOFORUS KONSTANTINOU
LEOFORUS STASINOU
STA BOUMPOULINA
SANDROU
PINDAROU
AKRITA
DIGENI
AKROTA
LEOFORUS EVAGOROU
LEOFORUS ARCHIEPISKOPOU MAKARIOU III
THEM
DERVI
LEOFORUS GRIVA DIGENI
LEOFORUS GRIVA DIGENI
DIMOSTHENI
SEVERI
LEOFORUS VYRONOS
KANARI
KATSONI
CHR MATSI
LEOFORUS KYRIAKOU
DIGENI
LEOFORUS ARCHIEPISKOPOU MAKARIOU III
LEOFORUS
KARPENISIOU
KALLIPOLEOS
SALA MINOS
LARNAKOS
AG ANDREOU
LEOFORUS P KAPOTA
Koral
BAF CADD
GİRNE CADD
İnanımat Şok
ERMU CADD
CADD
CADD
LEOFORUS KENNEDY
GLAFKOU
AKROPOLEOS

126

A
B
C
D
E
F

1
2
3
4

Notes

Notes